PHILIP ALLAN
LITERATURE GUIDE
FOR GCSE

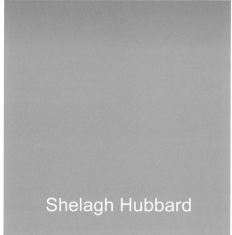

PRIDE AND PREJUDICE
JANE AUSTEN

Shelagh Hubbard

With thanks to Jeanette Weatherall for reviewing the manuscript of this book.

Philip Allan Updates, an imprint of Hodder Education, an Hachette UK company, Market Place, Deddington, Oxfordshire OX15 0SE

Orders

Bookpoint Ltd, 130 Milton Park, Abingdon, Oxfordshire OX14 4SB
tel: 01235 827720
fax: 01235 400454
e-mail: uk.orders@bookpoint.co.uk
Lines are open 9.00 a.m.–5.00 p.m., Monday to Saturday, with a 24-hour message answering service. You can also order through the Philip Allan Updates website: www.philipallan.co.uk

© Philip Allan Updates 2010
ISBN 978-1-4441-1027-2
First printed 2010

Impression number 5 4 3 2 1
Year 2015 2014 2013 2012 2011 2010

Cover photo reproduced by permission of TopFoto
Printed in Spain

Hachette UK's policy is to use papers that are natural, renewable and recyclable products and made from wood grown in sustainable forests. The logging and manufacturing processes are expected to conform to the environmental regulations of the country of origin.

Contents

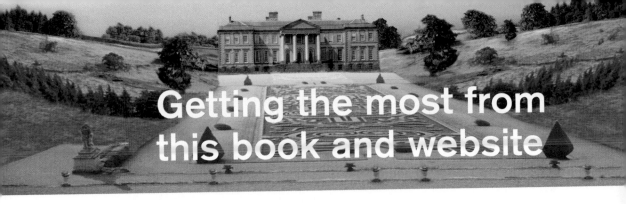

Getting the most from this book and website

You may find it useful to read sections of this guide when you need them, rather than reading it from start to finish. For example, you may find it helpful to read the *Context* section before you start reading the novel, or to read the *Plot and structure* section in conjunction with the novel — whether to back up your first reading of it at school or college or to help you revise. The sections relating to assessments will be especially useful in the weeks leading up to the exam.

The following features have been used throughout this guide.

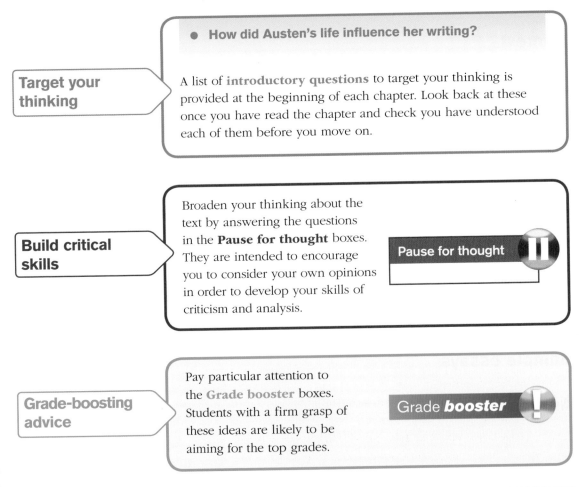

- **How did Austen's life influence her writing?**

Target your thinking

A list of **introductory questions** to target your thinking is provided at the beginning of each chapter. Look back at these once you have read the chapter and check you have understood each of them before you move on.

Build critical skills

Broaden your thinking about the text by answering the questions in the **Pause for thought** boxes. They are intended to encourage you to consider your own opinions in order to develop your skills of criticism and analysis.

Pause for thought ❚❚

Grade-boosting advice

Pay particular attention to the **Grade booster** boxes. Students with a firm grasp of these ideas are likely to be aiming for the top grades.

Grade *booster* ❗

PHILIP ALLAN LITERATURE GUIDE **FOR GCSE**

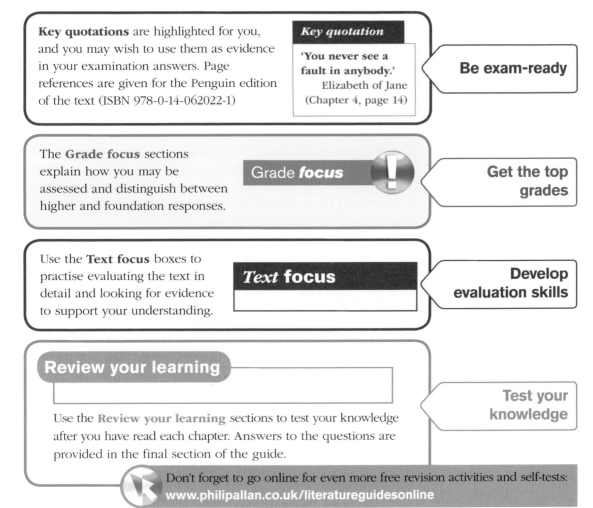

Key quotations are highlighted for you, and you may wish to use them as evidence in your examination answers. Page references are given for the Penguin edition of the text (ISBN 978-0-14-062022-1)

> **Key quotation**
>
> 'You never see a fault in anybody.'
> Elizabeth of Jane
> (Chapter 4, page 14)

Be exam-ready

The **Grade focus** sections explain how you may be assessed and distinguish between higher and foundation responses.

Grade *focus* !

Get the top grades

Use the **Text focus** boxes to practise evaluating the text in detail and looking for evidence to support your understanding.

Text **focus**

Develop evaluation skills

Review your learning

Use the **Review your learning** sections to test your knowledge after you have read each chapter. Answers to the questions are provided in the final section of the guide.

Test your knowledge

Don't forget to go online for even more free revision activities and self-tests:
www.philipallan.co.uk/literatureguidesonline

Approaching the text

A novel is, above all, a narrative. A large part of the storyteller's art is to make you want to find out what happens and to keep you reading to the end. To study *Pride and Prejudice,* and to enjoy it, you need to keep a close track of the events that take place. This guide will help you to do that, but you may also benefit from keeping your own notes.

Any novel consists of much more than its events. Although you need to know the story well to get a good grade in your GCSE exam, if all you do is simply retell the story you will not get a high mark. You also need to keep track of a number of other features.

- You need to **understand the characters** — how does Austen let us know what they are like? Notice what they say and do, and what other people say about them. Think about why they behave in the way they do — their motives — and what the author has to say about this. Think about how they compare with each other and the reasons why the author has included them in the story. After all they are not real people: they have been created for particular purposes.
- You need to **take notice of the setting** of the novel — where and when the events take place — and how this influences the story.
- As you read on, you will notice **themes** — the ideas explored by the author. You may find it easier to consider these while not actually reading the book, especially if you discuss them with other people.
- You should try to become aware of the **style** of the novel — this means *how* the author tells the story.

All these aspects of the novel are dealt with in this guide, but you should always try to work on your own ideas. High grades come from your own responses, so use this guide to get you thinking.

Watching the film

There have been several stage and musical productions of *Pride and Prejudice* since its first radio broadcast by the BBC in 1924. More recently there have been television adaptations very much in tune with the modern viewer, notably one scripted by Fay Weldon in 1980 and another by Andrew Davies in 1995 including the memorable scene in which Darcy confronts Elizabeth at Pemberley half dressed and wet through.

Film versions include one directed by Robert Z. Leonard (1940) and most recently by Joe Wright (2005). Film spin-offs include the 'updated' version *Bridget Jones's Diary* (which itself began as a novel) with a modern city-dwelling, single woman as heroine. Also interesting is the Bollywood treatment of the novel in *Bride and Prejudice* (directed by Gurinder Chadha in 2004), which might inspire you to reflect on how some modern British families' lives still have a central focus on finding suitable husbands for their daughters.

Watch and enjoy these television adaptations and films and use them to add to your interpretation of the novel, but do beware of writing about them as if they were Austen's original work. Austen was writing about her own world and its concerns, not creating costume drama.

Context

- **What is 'context'?**
- **How did Austen's life influence her writing?**
- **How much are historical events an influence on the novel?**
- **How was life for women of Austen's social class different from the life of modern women?**
- **Is the novel still relevant to modern readers?**

The **context** of a novel means the circumstances in which it was written — the social, historical and literary factors that influenced what the author wrote.

The social and historical context of *Pride and Prejudice* is important: Austen's world was very different from ours, two centuries later. She focuses on a privileged class of English society and she writes from a woman's perspective about relationships between her characters rather than constructing an action-packed plot. The book went through various versions at the end of the eighteenth and beginning of the nineteenth century and was eventually published in 1813.

Jane Austen

The most important thing to know about Jane Austen's life is that she was a writer. However, there is interest in knowing something about her and the events of the world she lived in. Reading this section will help you to make better sense of aspects of the social world of *Pride and Prejudice* that are different from today's world.

TopFoto

Facts and letters

Information about Austen's life is limited and we know only a few facts about her childhood. As an adult, she was a great letter writer, so there are some details about her private life, particularly from the letters she sent to her sister, Cassandra, but many of these were destroyed.

Jane Austen

Memoirs and biography

Relatives' memories of their childless maiden aunt provide (probably censored and biased) accounts of her life. In 1869, her nephew, James Edward Austen-Leigh wrote *A Memoir of Jane Austen*. In the twentieth century many professional biographers have written about her. Recently, the film *Becoming Jane* (2007) presented an imaginative account of her romantic life.

But what are the facts?

Jane Austen was born on 16 December 1775 and died on 18 July 1817. Her parents were George and Cassandra Austen and she was the seventh of eight children born between 1765 and 1779. She had six brothers and one older sister, Cassandra. Her father was a clergyman in Steventon, Hampshire, and, at times, a teacher. Although the family was on the fringes of the social class known as 'gentry', they did not have a great deal of money — like the Bennets in *Pride and Prejudice*.

Austen was offered more education than most girls at that time. She did attend school for a while, but most of her education took place in her father's library (a little like Elizabeth Bennet) alongside her brothers and extended beyond sewing, music, French and good manners, which girls of her social class usually received in school.

In her teens Austen began to write plays, poems and stories. Some of these still exist in notebooks she copied out at the time. Her satirical sense of humour begins to show in this early work.

As Austen grew up, she stayed at home while her brothers married and began families of their own. Neither of the sisters married and it was not uncommon for women of their background to opt for a single life rather than risk a less than perfect marriage and death in childbirth. Nevertheless, Austen's letters to Cassandra hint at a romance with a man called Tom Lefroy, but this came to nothing as neither had any inherited money to make marriage possible.

Austen wrote letters all the time and, sometimes under the cover of writing letters, the six novels that made her reputation as a great English author. In the mid-1790s she began a novel she called *Lady Susan*, which became *Sense and Sensibility*. Before she reached the age of 21 she had written a second novel called *First Impressions*, which became *Pride and Prejudice*. Next came *Northanger Abbey*. Her father and brother Henry attempted to interest publishers in her writing, but it was more than ten years before anything was published.

In 1800 the family moved to the city of Bath, fashionable and more sophisticated than a Hampshire village. Although Austen wrote no novels during the six years she spent there, Bath is a setting found in many of her works. It was in Bath that she received her only proposal of marriage: from Harris Bigg-Wither, a man who sounds rather like a Mr Collins.

In 1805 Austen's father died so she, her mother and sister, now financially dependent on her brothers, moved to Southampton. In 1809 they settled in Chawton House, a property in a village on her brother Edward's estate. Here she lived for her last seven years, writing *Mansfield Park*, *Emma* and her final novel, *Persuasion*.

Finally publishers began to take an interest in her novels: *Sense and Sensibility* was published in 1811, followed by *Pride and Prejudice* in 1813, *Mansfield Park* in 1814 and *Emma* in 1815. The novels were popular and sold well.

In 1816, Austen became ill, though she continued to write until her death in 1817. Her final novel, *Persuasion* was published together with *Northanger Abbey* six months after her death. She was buried in Winchester Cathedral. Chawton House is now the home of the Jane Austen museum.

The role of women

Women and writing

The novel, a fictional story about invented people, was an innovation of the eighteenth century and most early novelists were male. Women generally did not have the same education as their brothers. They were taught to read and became enormous consumers of novels, but generally did not learn to write well enough for publication. There were women writing before Austen and no doubt she read the work of Frances Burney and Amelia Opie, among others, but these books were not regarded as 'great writing' in the class of male novelists.

Women and the public world

It was hard for women at this time to have their writing taken seriously. They were not meant to take an interest in the public world of great events and politics and, although many did, it was certainly not appropriate for women to write about such things. It is said that Austen often physically hid her novel writing under the pretence of writing a letter if interrupted by an outsider.

Even though Austen's subject matter was acceptable, making her writing public was not an easy task and it was her father and brother who tried to find a publisher for her novels. Women of her class did write, but it was usually private: personal journals and letters to friends and family — nothing intended for publication.

> **Pause for thought**
>
> One novelist who certainly influenced Austen was Mrs Radcliffe. Her supernatural 'gothic' novels were popular at the time — the kind of lending library books Mr Collins is so critical about. *The Mysteries of Udolpho* was the direct inspiration for Austen's *Northanger Abbey*, which is a parody of the gothic genre.

Later in the nineteenth century women who wrote novels of ideas sometimes published under men's names (for instance, Mary Ann Evans wrote under the name George Eliot) rather than face outrage at 'unsuitable' subject matter.

Pause for thought

Here are some key dates in history during Austen's life:

- 1775: Start of American war of independence
- 1783: Britain recognises the USA as an independent country
- 1789: French Revolution
- 1792: *A Vindication of the Rights of Women* by Mary Wollstonecraft is published
- 1793: France declares war on Britain
- 1798: *Lyrical Ballads*, Romantic poetry by Wordsworth and Coleridge, is published
- 1801: Britain and Ireland joined by the Act of Union
- 1805: Nelson's victory at the battle of Trafalgar
- 1811: Luddite riots in protest at the Industrial Revolution — machinery in factories smashed
- 1814: Stephenson presents his steam locomotive to the public
- 1815: Napoleon defeated at Waterloo

How much do you learn about such events from reading *Pride and Prejudice*?

Austen's world of the private and personal

The world of Austen's novels is the private and domestic one, inhabited by women like herself. She never writes about the lives of servants (though they are there in the households she describes). She rarely writes about men in a situation where there are no women present: how would she know about that?

Austen never moves out into the world of public events. During the early 1800s, there was trouble in Ireland and war between England and France, yet in *Pride and Prejudice* the only reference to the military preparations against invasion by Napoleon's troops is the red-coated captains and sergeants who provide romantic interest for the young ladies, for example Mr Wickham (Chapter 15, pages 58–59).

The Regency world

The Regency is the period of English history between the Georgians and the Victorians and takes in Austen's adult life, from the mid-1790s until the late 1830s. The name comes from the Prince Regent who took the throne from his father, King George III, in 1811 (when King George was declared unfit to rule) to his death in 1820.

Distinctive changes in literature, social life, fashion and architecture had been taking place all over the country from the late eighteenth century onwards.

The Romantic movement

At the end of the eighteenth century literary conventions were moving away from literature that was concerned with intellectual argument and rational understanding towards writing that described strong emotions as a valid source of meaningful human experience. This is now known as the Romantic movement and it involved artists and musicians as well as writers.

Untamed nature and spontaneous emotions became the subjects of Romantic poets like Wordsworth, Shelley and Byron, whose work was both fashionable and popular in Austen's time.

A culture of revolution and freedom

Writers also celebrated events like the French Revolution, which altered thinking about class and equality, power and freedom.

Books about politics and philosophy appeared on both sides of the Channel with new ideas — even the beginnings of a proposal that women might be equal to men. Austen resisted being swept away by excitement: the balance and judgement she promotes in the novels is her response. She is wary of the Romantic attitude that emotion is a truer response to life's events than rational thought. It is clear in her writing that characters whose hearts rule their heads end up in disastrous circumstances — as does Lydia Bennet.

Yet she allows her heroines to be unconventional in some ways. Elizabeth Bennet walks to Netherfield, hatless, and looking 'almost wild' when she arrives. She speaks to Darcy (and even the intimidating Lady Catherine) as an intellectual equal, a radical thing to do considering the social distance between them.

> **Pause for thought**
>
> Austen's style and views are said to have been drawn from the writers of the eighteenth century — earlier authors like Johnson and Swift who wrote witty and logical social commentary. As you read *Pride and Prejudice*, ask yourself whether this is the influence you see or whether there is evidence of Romantic ideas in the characters and events she creates.

Grade *focus*

Knowing about debates that were going on and writers and thinkers who influenced an author will raise your grade. Each exam board places different amounts of weight on each Assessment Objective. Edexcel, CCEA and particularly WJEC give marks to understanding of context, and the questions set reflect this.

For a C or B grade, your writing needs to show you are *aware* of historical, social and cultural influences. To raise your grade to an A you need to *comment on and explain the importance* of contextual information, in other words, to demonstrate how information from this section helps you to understand and interpret Austen's novel.

To reach the top grades you also have to show you are aware of 'the literary heritage'. This means how a particular novel fits in with other writing done before and after it.

Elizabeth (Jennifer Ehle) and Darcy
(Colin Firth) in the 1995 BBC production

Fashion

The stiff clothing and powdered wigs of the early Georgians contrasted with the looser clothes worn in Regency times. This is shown in the clothes worn in film adaptations of Austen's novels: soft, flowing empire-line muslin dresses for women, and natural hair for both sexes. The same underlying idea of celebrating freedom and nature, as opposed to the previous generation's more formal and sophisticated approach to life, is therefore reflected in how people dressed.

Architecture

Buildings showing architectural designs from all kinds of exotic places reflected their owners' education and travel abroad, while extravagant spending on property reflected a man's wealth, taste and status. The Prince Regent's Brighton Pavilion (built in Indian style 1815–22) is an example of this. It was also fashionable for gentlemen to make alterations to their country houses in the manner of ancient Greek and Roman architecture. In town, Regency terraced houses and the crescents of London and Bath were built in this classical style.

There were some appalling slum buildings (and terrible poverty) in the cities of England, but that was outside Austen's world.

Social class

Key quotation

'Do let the portraits of your uncle and aunt Philips be placed in the gallery at Pemberley. Put them next to your great-uncle the judge. They are in the same profession, you know; only in different lines.'

Caroline Bingley sneers about Elizabeth's socially inferior relatives to entertain Darcy (Chapter 10, page 43)

Rigid social class barriers in England began to break down in the eighteenth century, as people whose wealth was based on ownership of land (the traditional aristocracy, like Darcy) were joined by people who had made their money in trade and industry. Rich middle-class people could buy education for their sons to turn them into gentlemen (like Mr Bingley). They could even buy titles from old landed families who had fallen on hard times. A pretty girl whose family had made money might make a good marriage to an aristocrat who needed cash to maintain his ancestral home. Yet snobbery still existed against those who had earned rather than inherited money. The most severe snobbery could be shown by the children of the parents who had earned the money. The Bingley sisters are an example of this.

Changes in attitude were certainly taking place in enlightened circles. In *Pride and Prejudice* demonstrations of the blurring of social divisions include:

● Darcy's friendship with Bingley

- the growth in his respect for the middle-class Gardiners
- his rift with his aristocratic aunt, Lady Catherine, when he chooses Elizabeth Bennet as his wife

Income and inheritance

Upper-class marriages were often based on considerations about money. There are examples of this in the novel. Austen's work is modern (even revolutionary) in her portrayal of the ideal marriage being between individuals who love and respect each other. These matches are 'suitable' (based on secure finances) but they involve romantic love in the modern sense of the word. Sometimes Austen's work is revolutionary in that she shows love overturning conventional expectations about age gaps or social distance.

The institution of marriage was important to the rich middle class and the gentry because all the family money, land and property was inherited by the eldest son. Girls did not usually inherit, unless there were no male heirs at all (Lady Catherine and her daughter). In fact women rarely had any independent income. Daughters depended on their father's incomes, wives on their husbands and unmarried women on their brothers or more distant family. It was almost impossible for a middle-class woman to find any respectable way of earning her own living and there were no state benefits in those days. Marriage was therefore the only way to escape dependence on the family or poverty.

The main reason for giving almost all the land and wealth to one child was to stop great estates being broken up. There was a strict order of male inheritance: the eldest son got the big house and most of the fortune that went with it. The next son was educated and prepared for the church (a nice house and some land would go with the job as in Mr Collins' case). Younger sons went into the army or sometimes became gentleman farmers.

If a family was rich enough, a father could give each of his children an income from the estate. In less wealthy families, the younger children had to make good marriages to ensure they had something to live on.

Entailment was a legal way of making sure houses and money went to a male. If there was no son, the nearest male relative would inherit. This is what has happened to Mr Bennet, who has no son. His cousin Mr Collins, not the Bennet sisters, will inherit Longbourn.

Etiquette: civility and manners

To a modern reader, the world of *Pride and Prejudice* seems like a foreign country, with its unspoken rules and expectations of how people should behave. The words 'gentleman' and 'civility' are repeated through the book, both carrying expectations of standards of behaviour.

Pause for thought

How rich is Darcy? You can work that out by comparing his annual income of £10,000 with the earnings of other classes of people in the year 1800. Mr Bennet has £2,000 a year. A merchant like Mr Gardiner would probably earn less than £1,000 a year. A shopkeeper might make a profit of £150 a year. A farm labourer would be paid less than £1 a week.

The opening chapters show how visits and introductions have to be carried out in a certain way. There are also rules about what is acceptable in conversation, between different ranks of society and between the sexes. Mrs Bennet, her sister, Mrs Philips, Mr Collins and Lydia all become embarrassments to Elizabeth and Jane because they fail to follow these rules.

Austen is concerned with matters of morality and constantly draws the reader's attention to rude or hypocritical behaviour. We are required to judge whether the expectations and standards themselves are valid and useful, as well as make judgements about how the characters in the book measure up to the expectations society places upon them.

Pause for thought

Now and then — what else was different?

- Cities were smaller and there were fewer towns. Most people lived in villages in the country.
- No electricity — houses were lit with whale-oil lamps, or, if you were rich enough, candles.
- No television or recorded music — entertainment was games of cards, local dances, playing and singing your own music, or, for the educated, reading.
- Transport — no trains, cars or planes: journeys were on foot or by horse. Roads were bad and travelling was slow.
- Communication — no phones or internet. Letters were the only way to send news and 'the post' was a horse-drawn carriage.

Comparison with modern times

You may not earn marks in a GCSE exam for being able to compare the social context of *Pride and Prejudice* with that of modern times, but it will help you to understand the novel more fully and to gain a better understanding of the characters. The love story of Darcy and Elizabeth has proved to have enduring appeal and is the blueprint for modern romance fiction, although today's writers include more description of physical affection. You might have noticed that the characters in Austen's novels do not touch each other, except on the dance floor.

Review your learning

(Answers are given on page 90)

1 What is meant by the 'context' of a novel?
2 How long did Austen live? Does this surprise you? How many novels did she have published?
3 How did the Regency period get its name? How did it contrast with the Georgian period?
4 Identify three important historical events that happened during Austen's lifetime. How are these events reflected in her writing?
5 From what you know so far, does the novel seem relevant to readers in modern Britain?

More interactive questions and answers online.

Plot and structure

- **What are the obstacles to Darcy and Elizabeth's relationship?**
- **Which events draw them together?**
- **How does the passage of time underpin and reflect the development of their relationship?**

Pride and Prejudice is a lengthy novel of 61 chapters and nearly 300 pages. To aid your understanding of events, this guide divides the plot into eight sections.

Chapters 1–12: Bingley's first month at Netherfield

- The Bennet family reacts to news of their new neighbour.
- Bingley and Darcy meet the Bennet girls at the Meryton assembly.
- Darcy admires Elizabeth during a visit to Lucas Lodge.
- Jane and Elizabeth stay at Netherfield.
- Darcy's interest in Elizabeth grows.

Darcy (Matthew Macfadyen) and Bingley (Simon Woods) in the 2005 film

The novel opens by introducing us to Mr and Mrs Bennet and their five daughters as they discuss the news that a single, wealthy young man, Mr Bingley, has rented a local estate, Netherfield Park. Mrs Bennet sees him as a potential husband for her eldest daughter.

Having visited the Bennets, Bingley goes to London and returns to the house with his two sisters, Caroline Bingley and Louisa Hurst, Louisa's husband, and his very wealthy friend, Mr Darcy, all of whom make their first appearance at a public ball in Meryton.

Text focus

Read Chapter 3, pages 10–12, from 'Mr Bingley was good looking and gentle-manlike' to '…Longbourn, the village where they lived…'

● Remember that the novel's original title was *First Impressions* as you read the description of how the girls first meet Bingley and Darcy at the Meryton assembly.

● How things appear and how the reality may differ is an important theme, and so is the unreliability of general gossip. Both are reflected in this chapter, for example: '…a report soon followed, that Mr Bingley was to bring twelve ladies and seven gentlemen with him to the assembly' (page 10).

How many examples of these themes can you find in the extract?

Over the next fortnight the two households meet on several occasions, memorably at Lucas Lodge where Darcy is shown to have changed his mind that none of the local girls is worth dancing with, and is actually attracted to Elizabeth. He is surprised when he invites her to dance and she refuses.

Jane's closeness to the Bingleys grows and she is delighted by an invitation to Netherfield. Her mother sends her on horseback, hoping that poor weather means she will have to stay overnight. The plan works better than Mrs Bennet could have wished: Jane is soaked, catches cold and has to remain there in bed for a couple of days. Elizabeth, to the horror of the Bingley sisters, walks three miles through the fields to look after her sister, arriving with muddy feet and messy hair.

While Jane recovers, the sisters spend the best part of a week at Netherfield. Darcy now begins to admire Elizabeth's spirited character as well as her looks — and Caroline Bingley is most put out.

Text focus

Read Chapter 10, pages 42–44 from 'Mrs Hurst sang with her sister…' to the end of the chapter. Note how cleverly Austen switches point of view here:

● from Elizabeth's — 'She hardly knew how to suppose that she could be an object of admiration to so great man; and yet that he should look at her because he disliked her, was still more strange.'

- to Darcy's — '…there was a mixture of sweetness and archness in her manner which made it difficult for her to affront anybody; and Darcy had never been so bewitched by any woman as he was by her.'
- to Caroline's: — 'Miss Bingley saw, or suspected enough to be jealous'

Chapters 13–20: introducing Mr Collins and Mr Wickham

- Mr Bennet tells the family of Mr Collins' plans to visit.
- Mr Collins arrives at Longbourn and Mr Wickham is spotted in Meryton.
- Mrs Philips holds a supper party that both young men attend.
- Bingley holds the long-promised ball at Netherfield.
- Mr Collins proposes marriage to Elizabeth and she rejects him.

Mr Bennet informs the family that he has been in communication with his cousin, Mr Collins, and that this young man, who is destined to inherit their estate, is coming to stay. Collins' letter marks him out as '…a mixture of servility and self-importance…' (page 52) and this is confirmed when he arrives and immediately assures them he intends to make an offer of marriage to one of his cousins.

Elizabeth, Kitty and Lydia walk into Meryton with Collins where they meet Wickham. Elizabeth is attracted to him and is intrigued by his reaction to a chance meeting with Darcy. Mrs Bennet's sister, Aunt Philips, invites the group to a supper party where Elizabeth spends much time talking to Wickham. He tells her the history of the breakdown of his relationship with the Darcy family.

Text focus

Read Chapter 16, pages 62–65 from 'Mr Wickham did not play at whist…' to '"…He deserves to be publicly disgraced."'

- How were Wickham's and Darcy's fathers acquainted? What promise does Wickham claim was made to him?
- Elizabeth's pleasure in sharing her bad opinion of Darcy and his pride is much in evidence. Should she so easily believe Wickham's version of Darcy's failure to keep his father's promise?
- Should a new acquaintance be so open in revealing his private business? Could there be another reason for the quarrel between the two men?

Pause for thought

By the time Elizabeth leaves Netherfield to go home, Darcy has resolved to control his feelings. Do you think the stay has altered her opinion of him?

Grade *booster*

Austen's introduction of Wickham into the story influences the development of the plot. He hardens Elizabeth's prejudice against Darcy, making her less receptive to his attentions. He also makes it less likely that she would consider any relationship with the unattractive Mr Collins. Demonstrating understanding of the subtext in this way will get you to the B grade.

The Bennet sisters wait impatiently for the long-promised ball at Netherfield. On their arrival, Elizabeth is disappointed to find that Wickham is not there. She is then surprised and irritated to be invited to dance by Darcy, with whom she has an uncomfortable conversation about his treatment of Wickham, although no name is mentioned. As the evening progresses she is embarrassed by the behaviour of her family (see *Characterisation*, pages 38–40). Next morning, further discomfort is caused by Collins' proposal of marriage.

Elizabeth dances with Bingley at the ball in the 1995 BBC production

Text focus

Read Chapter 19, pages 85–86 From "'Believe me my dear Miss Elizabeth…'" to "'…impossible for me to do otherwise than decline them.'"

- Consider the order of the reasons Collins gives for wishing to marry her. Why is this a particularly insulting way to begin?
- Can you find any evidence for the 'violence of [his] affection' for Elizabeth? What seems to be the personal reason for his wish to marry Elizabeth?

Grade *booster*

Note Austen's use of irony (see page 59), in that we interpret Mr Collins' words in a different sense from what is said. Note also Mr Bennet's ironical response to the proposal on page 90: 'Your mother will never see you again if you do *not* marry Mr Collins, and I will never speak you again if you *do*.' Discussion of language techniques allows you to demonstrate your understanding, or evaluation, of the effect of your quoted evidence. This will raise your grade.

Chapters 21–29: motivations for marriage

- The Bingleys leave for London.
- Mr Collins proposes to Charlotte Lucas and is accepted.
- Jane suffers separation from Bingley; Elizabeth comforts her.
- The Gardiners stay at Longbourn for Christmas.
- Jane returns to London with the Gardiners.
- Charlotte and Collins marry and invite Elizabeth to stay at Hunsford.
- Two months later, Elizabeth accompanies Sir William and Maria Lucas to London then Hunsford.

Two days later the Bingleys leave for London and Jane is upset. Elizabeth's reaction is diverted by two events. First, Wickham is back in Meryton. Second, to everyone's astonishment, two days after his proposal to Elizabeth, Collins proposes to Charlotte Lucas and is accepted.

Text **focus**

Read the closing scene of Chapter 22, pages 100–01 from 'The possibility of Mr Collins's fancying himself in love…'
- Consider how different characters react to Charlotte's acceptance of Collins.
- Now look at the positive advantages Charlotte expects from the marriage.
- Do you agree with Elizabeth that it is impossible that Charlotte will be happy?

Austen sets slower development of the plot against the background of the cold, grey, protracted English winter. The season reflects the suspended emotions of the main characters. Almost a month passes and Caroline Bingley's letters further upset Jane, repeating that there is no intention to return to Netherfield.

Mrs Bennet's brother and his wife (the Gardiners) arrive at Longbourn for Christmas and Wickham is a constant guest. Mrs Gardiner is from Derbyshire and knows of the Darcy and Wickham families, though she has no knowledge of the events that caused the two young men to fall out. She warns Elizabeth that a relationship with Wickham is impractical as neither has money to finance a marriage. Elizabeth draws a parallel between her own and Charlotte's circumstances.

Christmas over, the Gardiners return to London and Jane goes with them. Charlotte and Collins marry in the New Year, promising that Elizabeth may visit Hunsford in March.

Jane, hearing nothing from the Bingley sisters, pays them a visit at the Hursts' townhouse. They treat her coldly and, rudely, do not return her

call for a month. It is clear to Elizabeth, when she reads of this in Jane's letter, that they have lost interest in her.

Spring arrives and the action of the plot begins to quicken. Elizabeth discovers that Wickham has transferred his affections to a Miss King, who has just inherited £10,000 a year. Sir William and Maria Lucas set off with Elizabeth to visit the Collinses. They travel from Hertfordshire via the Gardiners' London house.

Mrs Gardiner discusses Wickham's change of affections and Elizabeth compares his motivation to Charlotte's, saying he has a need to consider finance when choosing a spouse. Mrs Gardiner invites Elizabeth on a summer tour 'to the lakes' and Elizabeth accepts.

From London the Lucases and Elizabeth travel on to Hunsford in Kent where Collins and Charlotte take pleasure in showing them the Parsonage.

Pause for thought

The London addresses Grosvenor Street and Gracechurch Street are real, the Hursts being situated in Mayfair, a fashionable West End area, the Gardiners in the East End, less affluent and more associated with trade and business. Mrs Gardiner comments on the social distance between the families: 'We live in so different a part of town, all our connections are so different…' (page 112). What opinion does Elizabeth assume Darcy would hold of her relatives' home?

Grade *booster*

There is comedy in this section of the novel deriving from the satirical caricatures of both Mr Collins and Lady Catherine. Demonstrating that you understand what satire is (see page 60) and how it achieves its effects on the reader is an excellent way of showing you can analyse the sub-text of the novel — a B-grade skill.

Text *focus*

Read Chapter 28, pages 123–24 from 'Elizabeth was prepared to see him in his glory…' to '…he must be often forgotten.'
- Has Charlotte achieved her expectations of marriage?
- What disadvantages are there in having Collins as a husband?
- What positive aspects are there?

Within days they are invited to Rosings to dine with the woman we already know from Wickham as Darcy's proud aunt, Lady Catherine de Bourgh, and her daughter, Anne, who Caroline Bingley has implied will be Darcy's wife.

Chapters 30–34: Darcy's courting of Elizabeth

- Sir William returns to Longbourn.
- Easter approaches and Darcy and his cousin, Colonel Fitzwilliam Darcy, visit Rosings.
- They visit the parsonage regularly and pay attention to Elizabeth.
- Colonel Fitzwilliam and Elizabeth discuss his financial considerations about marriage.
- Darcy unexpectedly asks Elizabeth to marry him. She refuses.

Easter approaches, a time of year associated with renewed life and hope, and there is talk of Darcy visiting Rosings. Elizabeth assumes he will be with the same party as at Netherfield, so it is a surprise when Darcy arrives accompanied only by his cousin, Colonel Fitzwilliam. It is more of a surprise when the two young men return Collins' welcoming visit by calling at Hunsford the very next day. Charlotte guesses that Elizabeth is the attraction.

Text **focus**

This section is a key turning point in the plot and requires serious attention. You are recommended to read Chapters 30–34 in their entirety. Pay close attention to:

- clues that Darcy is seriously attracted to Elizabeth
- evidence that Darcy is seeking out Elizabeth's company to learn more about her
- evidence that other characters guess his feelings, even though Elizabeth is blind to them

Darcy begins to seek out occasions to speak to Elizabeth on her own. The first could be an accident: he visits the Parsonage when the Lucas sisters are out. However, further meetings occur as Elizabeth takes solitary walks. She cannot understand how they keep meeting because she has told him about her walks to warn him away from her, but the reader can see that Darcy is actively pursuing her company.

Elizabeth's growing closeness with Colonel Fitzwilliam comes to an abrupt end when he reminds her that younger sons do not have financial independence and that he would not be able to consider taking a wife who did not bring a fortune with her. His words echo Wickham's action (his pursuit of Miss King and her money), though his behaviour is a good deal more gentlemanly.

Pause for thought

Darcy is taking risks with conventional ideas about correct behaviour here. According to the moral code of the time, a single man and woman should not meet and talk together without a chaperone. This is why their meetings have to appear to be accidental, although they are clearly intentional on his part. How are we to judge this? Is he unconcerned about how others may condemn Elizabeth? Or are we to read this as a 'wild' streak in him, a little like Elizabeth's 'wild' walk to Netherfield?

He reveals that Darcy has spoken of how he separated Bingley from a romance because of '…very strong objections against the lady' (page 145), though, ironically, he has no idea that it is Elizabeth and her family who would be offended by hearing this.

Thus the circumstances of Darcy's proposal mirror those of Collins': she prefers another man and, once again, he has been the source of information which reinforces her prejudice against Darcy.

Read Chapter 34, pages 147–48 (the proposal) from 'While settling this point…' to '"…But it is of small importance."'

- List the reasons Darcy has 'struggled' against his feelings for Elizabeth. Note how he stresses that his love and admiration have overcome his reservations.
- Compare this with Collins' proposal. Would it be fair to say that Elizabeth would have found it more difficult to reject Darcy without the prejudice she has built up against him?
- Also consider why Austen chose to write Collins' proposal in his words, while here she paraphrases much of what Darcy says. The possible effect of this is to place the reader firmly in Elizabeth's shoes. Where does the account reflect her response rather than his words?

The chapter ends with each of the couple in a state of considerable agitation. Elizabeth's is conveyed by the author. Darcy's, the reader is left to guess at.

Chapters 35–42: reflections and changes of heart

- Darcy gives Elizabeth a letter of apology; he and Colonel Fitzwilliam leave.
- Elizabeth reflects on Darcy's words, beginning to question her judgements.
- She returns to Longbourn, via London, with Jane.
- Lydia wishes to follow Wickham's regiment to Brighton; eventually her father agrees to this.
- Elizabeth's planned trip to the north is postponed and shortened.
- The destination is changed from the Lakes to Derbyshire; the party decides to visit Pemberley.

An important development occurs immediately after Elizabeth rejects Darcy's proposal. Austen includes a lengthy letter from him, '…two sheets of letter-paper, written quite through, in a very close hand' (page 152), from which the reader has a first real opportunity to judge his character from his own viewpoint.

Read Chapter 35, pages 152–55.
- Consider the first part of Darcy's letter and form your opinion of his motives for separating his friend Bingley from Jane.
- List the three reasons he gives for this and add your own judgement as to whether he was right or wrong to act as he did.

Now read Darcy's account of Wickham's story (pages 155–58). Remind yourself how it differs from what Wickham told Elizabeth about:

- the events that led up to Darcy refusing him the living at Pemberley
- the compensation Darcy gave instead of the position
- Wickham's wasteful lifestyle after this
- his attempted seduction of Darcy's 15-year-old sister

Finally, read the opening of Chapter 36, page 159. Consider Elizabeth's first reaction on reading this letter and list all the moments when her prejudice against Darcy leads her to wish to disbelieve every word he wrote.

The reader is shown how Elizabeth gradually changes her opinion of Darcy. Initially, she resolves not to reread the letter, but in the end it is almost falling apart from being read and reread. If you have ever received an important letter, or text or e-mail, you will understand this. She reflects upon and reinterprets what Darcy has said over and over again. She realises how his deceptive charm blinded her to Wickham's bad character and begins to understand the true character of Darcy, which prejudice about his assumed pride has prevented her from seeing till now. She eventually has a complete change of heart.

This is a major turning point: from here on Elizabeth will move closer and closer to her destiny, marriage with Darcy. Like Darcy, she begins to change for the better. In terms of development of the plot, only when that transformation of each is complete will they be ready to marry.

Elizabeth and Maria return to London, from where, with Jane, they travel to Longbourn. Austen sets up two elements of plot which will shape the concluding sections of the novel.

First, Lydia's silly, reckless character is brought to the fore. Elizabeth points out to her father the dangers of allowing her to follow the regiment to Brighton. Cynical Mr Bennet is sure she will come to no real harm, but it is obvious to the reader that she will not be effectively chaperoned by young Mrs Forster and that trouble is bound to follow.

Second, the Gardiner's long trip to the Lake District becomes impossible and Derbyshire is now their destination. Mrs Gardiner is delighted to have the chance to return to her childhood home and a visit to Darcy's country house, Pemberley, is proposed, to Elizabeth's discomfort.

> **Key quotation**
>
> She grew absolutely ashamed of herself. Of neither Darcy nor Wickham could she think without feeling that she had been blind, partial, prejudiced, absurd.
> (Elizabeth, Chapter 36, page 162)

Chapters 43–48: love and loss at Pemberley

- Elizabeth visits Darcy's estate at Pemberley.
- Mr Darcy introduces Elizabeth to his sister.

- Elizabeth's feelings for Darcy continue to change.
- A letter from Jane breaks the news of Wickham and Lydia's elopement.
- The Gardiners and Elizabeth return in haste to Longbourn.
- Mr Bennet and Mr Gardiner search for the illicit lovers.

The visit to Pemberley is a crucial turning point in the development of Elizabeth's and Darcy's relationship. Austen rarely describes settings in detail. That she does so here is significant, for the descriptions also symbolise Darcy himself.

Grade *booster*

Austen's knowledge of landscapes celebrated by the Romantic movement in art and literature is reflected in this choice of settings: the power and wildness of the natural landscape rather than manmade surroundings. The Lake District has a close connection with Wordsworth, while the Derbyshire dales and peaks are near Byron's home area and were familiar to the Shelleys. Pemberley is an imaginary estate, said to be based on Chatsworth in Derbyshire. Comments on details of context like this mark out a top-grade answer.

Text focus

Read the following key passages of description and consider what they emphasise about Darcy's positive qualities:

- pages 187–88 — the exterior of the house and its grounds
- pages 188 and 191 — the interior of the house
- pages 191–92 — the description of Mr Darcy's portrait

Now read the whole of Chapter 43, pages 187–98. What does it tell you about Darcy's positive qualities?

Grade *booster*

In Chapter 43 symbolism is used to reflect Elizabeth's wish to explore the hidden parts of Darcy: his mind, his intellect. It may also work to suggest her interest in him physically. Understanding and exploring such a complex piece of symbolism will lead to a top grade.

Elizabeth's reflections on her changing judgement of Darcy are abruptly halted as she comes face to face with the man himself, to the embarrassment of both parties. Darcy greets her with 'perfect civility' explaining that he has come ahead of a house party, including the Bingleys, who will arrive the following day.

As Elizabeth continues her tour around the grounds she reflects on her changing emotions as she reaches 'a spot less adorned than any they had yet visited; and the valley, here contracted into a glen, allowed room only for the stream, and a narrow walk amidst the rough coppice-wood which bordered it. Elizabeth longed to explore its windings' (page 194).

Darcy invites Mr Gardiner to fish and asks Elizabeth if he may introduce his sister to her. He has learnt his lesson: his conduct is perfect, his manners those of a true gentleman. He has taken Elizabeth's criticisms of his haughty attitude to heart. He brings his sister to meet Elizabeth and she then entertains the ladies at Pemberley while Darcy organises a fishing party for the men. Elizabeth is reacquainted with the Bingleys and is pleased that Mr Bingley remembers the date of the Netherfield ball, the last time he saw Jane.

A dinner party is planned, but unfortunate events intervene: two letters from Jane arrive at the same time (the first having been misdirected) and Elizabeth reads them in sequence. Her worst fears have come to pass, for Lydia and Wickham have eloped.

Lydia (Jena Malone) and Wickham (Rupert Friend) in the 2005 film

Darcy finds Elizabeth after she has read Jane's letters. She is absolutely honest about the events and, although he seems most concerned for her welfare, he does not say much. Elizabeth interprets his silence as an end to their closeness. She is acutely aware of the scandal of Lydia's actions and assumes that Darcy will wish to have no more to do with her family. However, there is another way to interpret his silence: he experienced a similar shock when Wickham's plan to elope with his sister Georgiana was exposed. As the plot progresses, it becomes clear that his thoughts are less of himself and more of what he can do — not for Lydia or Wickham but for Elizabeth.

Pause for thought

The letters inject tension. The first says that Lydia and Wickham have run away to Scotland to marry. The second is shocking: they are living together in London and seem to have no plans to marry at all. Austen hints here at a world she could never decently describe. We only learn that Georgiana's corrupt companion, Mrs Younge, has again helped Wickham, this time to find lodgings. If Lydia had not been saved by marriage, this seamy side of London would have swallowed her up forever. There would have been no return to respectability for her.

The Gardiners and Elizabeth return to Longbourn, from where Mr Gardiner travels immediately to London to join Mr Bennet in his search for the couple. Austen now injects elements of satirical comedy into the story as Mrs Bennet frets that her husband may be killed in a duel with Wickham. There are also exaggerated contrasts of attitude in Lydia's thoughtless note explaining her departure to Mrs Forster ('I can hardly write for laughing', page 223) and Mr Collins' sanctimonious letter advising Mr Bennet to '...throw off your unworthy child...' (page 227).

Chapters 49–55: Darcy helps Lydia

- Lydia and Wickham are found in London.
- Mr Gardiner organises their marriage.
- Elizabeth discovers that Darcy is behind the arrangements.
- Bingley and Darcy return to Netherfield.
- Bingley proposes to Jane.

Letters between London and Longbourn now play an important part in relating events as Mr Gardiner searches for the runaway lovers. Within a few days they are found and financial arrangements are put in place to ensure their marriage. At first it seems that Wickham has more money than suspected when he agrees to marry Lydia if she is assured of £1,000 on her father's death and £100 a year until then. Mr Bennet accepts these terms with disbelief. He reminds the reader of Wickham's previous pursuit of wealthy heiresses when he expresses surprise that anything less than £10,000 would persuade Wickham to marry — the same sum as Miss King's tempting fortune. However, their future is settled and a visit to Longbourn is planned after their wedding and before they travel to Newcastle to Wickham's new army posting.

Lydia moves to the Gardiner's house for a fortnight to prepare for the wedding and Elizabeth is left with time on her hands to regret that Lydia's rash actions have brought an end to her chances of a relationship with Darcy. Now that hopes of marriage have been dashed, she reflects that this could have been the perfect match for her.

A great surprise, therefore, is Lydia's careless revelation that Darcy was present at her wedding. Letters pass between Mrs Gardiner and Elizabeth in which it becomes clear how much the Bennet family owe to Darcy (as the reader may have suspected for some time.)

- His knowledge of the circumstances of Wickham's planned elopement with his sister helped him to locate the couple.
- He bribed Wickham into marriage by:
  - paying off his debts (not for the first time)

    – buying him a commission in the regular army to remove him from
      the scene of the scandal in Brighton
    – doubling the sum of the settlement for Lydia to £2,000
    all done before the Gardiners knew where the couple was staying.

Mrs Gardiner's letter hints that Elizabeth surely knew this, and that the reason for Darcy's action can only be his feelings for her.

It is now almost a year since Bingley first rented Netherfield and news arrives that the house is being prepared for his return. Within days, Bingley and Darcy visit the Bennet family. A dinner party follows where the reader shares Elizabeth's frustration at being unable to speak to Darcy at any length.

He then leaves for London as Jane and Bingley's courtship proceeds — now with his blessing. More social visits follow during which Mrs Bennet makes an exhibition of herself in her attempts to leave the couple alone together. In the end she succeeds, Bingley proposes to Jane and she accepts.

Chapters 56–61: Darcy resumes his courtship of Elizabeth

- Lady Catherine de Bourgh disapproves of Darcy's rumoured engagement to Elizabeth.
- Mr Collins writes to reinforce Lady Catherine's disapproval.
- Bingley returns to Netherfield with Darcy.
- Elizabeth admits to Darcy that her feelings have changed.
- He reiterates his proposal of marriage and she accepts.
- The family is informed of the news and a summary of Elizabeth's married life concludes the novel.

A surprise visit to Longbourn from Lady Catherine moves the plot forward rapidly. She has had news via the Lucases and Charlotte not only of Bingley and Jane's engagement, but also that Darcy and Elizabeth's will follow. She is incensed at her plans for Anne being thwarted, and becomes even angrier when she cannot force Elizabeth to promise such an engagement will never happen. In fact, her visit has the reverse effect, awakening Elizabeth's hope of Darcy's continued feelings for her, though reminding her (and the reader) of all the obstacles of social rank that stand between them.

A letter from Collins to Mr Bennet advises Elizabeth to avoid Lady Catherine's displeasure. Mr Bennet's amusement in sharing the contents with Elizabeth, since he knows nothing of her changed feelings towards Darcy, causes her further discomfort.

Text focus

Read Chapter 58, pages 282–83. Upon Bingley's return with Darcy, all is quickly resolved. Elizabeth finds herself walking alone with Darcy and opens up the possibility of intimate discussion by thanking him for all he did to help Lydia. Notice how Austen chooses once again to write the proposal in reported speech rather than as dialogue. How much information is gained about the changes each has brought about in the other's character as they reflect upon the growth of their feelings for each other?

Pause for thought

This is the climax of the plot: the moment the reader has been waiting for. How did you respond to it? Did it happen as you expected? Was anything not included which you would have expected? If so, why do you think that is?

The plot is bought to a conclusion. Bingley and Jane are delighted to hear the news. Mr Bennet is first alarmed, but Elizabeth reassures him that she is not entering into a marriage that could lead to similar unhappiness to his own. Mrs Bennet rapidly overcomes her dislike for Darcy when she considers his wealth.

Letters are sent to acquaint others with the news and responses are summarised, from Lady Catherine's anger to Georgiana's four-page expression of pleasure. The wedding itself is not described.

The final chapter summarises to what extent the various couples in the novel 'live happily ever after'. Jane and Bingley settle conveniently '… within thirty miles…' (page 297) of Pemberley. Lydia and Wickham are helped to cope with their itinerant life of debt. Life at Pemberley is blessed with the happiness of Darcy and Elizabeth, friendship between Elizabeth and her sister-in-law, and the Darcys and the Gardiners. Eventually, Lady Catherine forgives them sufficiently to visit.

The passage of time

The events of the novel take place over slightly more than a year. You have to pay close attention to work this out as dates are infrequently mentioned, though days of the week are, and the time lapsing between events. Some timings are so precise, it gives the impression that Austen plotted her events on a calendar.

Grade *booster*

The seasons reflect Elizabeth's feelings for Darcy: through the autumn and winter, she is cold towards him, but after his spring proposal, her feelings change and she warms towards him, finally marrying at the end of the summer. This technique is used in many romantic novels. Understanding the symbolism of this narrative craft will take you to the highest grades.

The date of Mr Collins' visit gives a clue to the year — in 1799, 18 November fell on a Monday.

Month	Chapter	Events
1799 Sept	1–2	Bingley rents Netherfield, sends servants to prepare the house. By Michaelmas (29 Sept) has moved in
Oct	3–6	Meryton assembly, the Bennets visit Netherfield, four dinner parties, a gathering at Sir William Lucas' house
Nov	7–23	13 Nov, Jane goes to Netherfield and catches cold 14–17 Nov, Elizabeth joins her 18 Nov, Mr Collins arrives; 19 Nov, Wickham arrives 26 Nov, Netherfield ball; 28 Nov, Bingleys leave for London 27 Nov, Collins proposes to Elizabeth; 29 Nov, to Charlotte
Dec	23–26	Jane pines for Bingley 23 Dec, Gardiners arrive for Christmas then return to London with Jane
1800 Jan	26	2 Jan, Collins and Charlotte marry and leave for Hunsford. Jane in London, calls on the Bingley sisters
Feb	26	Caroline returns Jane's visit, Jane writes to Elizabeth
March	27–30	Mid-March, Elizabeth travels to London then Hunsford with the Lucases. Around 20 Mar, dinner with Lady Catherine
April	30–38	Early April, Darcy and Colonel Fitzwilliam arrive 13 Apr, Easter day and dinner at Rosings 14 Apr, Darcy visits Hunsford and speaks to Elizabeth alone 15–19 Apr, Darcy seeks opportunities to talk to Elizabeth Around 21 Apr, Darcy proposes; 22 Apr, gives Elizabeth the letter; 23 Apr, leaves 25 Apr, Elizabeth travels to London
May	39–41	Second week in May, Jane and Elizabeth home to Longbourn End of May, the regiment leaves for Brighton, with Lydia
June	42	Mid-June, Lydia's 16th birthday
July	42–48	About 22 July, visit to Pemberley. 23–24 July, socialising with the Darcys 25 July, Jane's letters about Lydia's elopement arrive almost a week after the event; Gardiners return to Longbourn, then to London with Mr Bennet 26 July–end July, Darcy to London to find the runaways
Aug	49–51	First letter from Gardiner: Mr Bennet is on his way home Second letter sent by express from Gardiner: the couple have been found. Received on 4 Aug Lydia stays with the Gardiners until the wedding End August/early Sept, Lydia and Wickham marry then stay with the Bennets for ten days
Sept	51–54	Early Sept, Elizabeth's letter to Mrs Gardiner about Darcy's presence at the wedding; 6 Sept, Mrs Gardiner replies; 8 Sept Elizabeth receives the letter Mid-Sept, news that the Bingleys return Weds or Thurs (24 or 25 Sept?) for the shooting 27 Sept, Darcy and Bingley visit, invited to dinner on Tues 30 Sept
Oct	55–60	Darcy to London; Bingley calls every day Around 6 Oct, Bingley proposes to Jane and is accepted Around 13 Oct, Lady Catherine calls; later that week, Darcy returns from London, visits and proposes to Elizabeth Next day Mr and Mrs Bennet are told the news
Late 1800	61	Weddings: date not stated

Review your learning

(Answers are given on p. 90)

1. When (month and year) does the novel start and end?

2. Use the *Plot and structure* summary and calendar on page 27 to list five major obstacles to Darcy and Elizabeth's developing love story.

3. Which three male characters are included as rivals for Elizabeth's affections?

4. Why are the Gardiners important to the plot?

5. What similar experience do Lydia Bennet and Georgiana Darcy have?

6. How do the seasons reflect the development of the plot?

7. Looking at the calendar above, which three months inject the greatest amounts of narrative tension into the story?

More interactive questions and answers online.

Characterisation

- **What is each character like?**
- **How does Austen reveal her characters to us?**
- **What evidence can we find to help us write about characters?**
- **What functions do characters serve in the novel?**
- **How will work on characters be assessed?**

Austen's methods of presenting characters can be a puzzle for new readers — she requires you to get under the surface of the evidence to interpret what it reveals about characters. There are four main types of evidence for character:

- **dialogue** — what the character says (or thinks) and what others say about them
- **actions** — what a character does
- **behaviour** in a social setting — words and actions relating to others
- **authorial comment** — how the author explains or judges the character

The character studies below look in detail at text from early on in the novel. They highlight evidence for you to follow up with your own reading and judgements.

Elizabeth Bennet

- is clever and educated
- can be articulate and witty
- has impeccable manners
- has strongly developed powers of judgement and a sense of morality
- is kind and loyal

The heroine is introduced into the story by her father as 'my little Lizzy', favoured above her elder sister, Jane, the conventionally pretty one, because she is the daughter with a good intellect, the one he treats almost like a son. First impressions of Elizabeth derive from conversations between her father and mother as they talk of the arrival of the eligible Mr Bingley in the neighbourhood.

Key quotation

'They have none of them much to recommend them,' replied he; 'they are all silly and ignorant like other girls; but Lizzy has something more of quickness than her sisters.'

Mr Bennet of his daughters (Chapter 1, page 6)

We also may judge her from what she says herself: her very first utterance shows her to be more adult and aware of social form than either of her parents seem to be:

'But you forget, mamma,' said Elizabeth, 'that we shall meet him at the assemblies, and that Mrs Long has promised to introduce him.'

'I do not believe Mrs Long will do any such thing. She has two nieces of her own. She is a selfish, hypocritical woman, and I have no opinion of her.'

(Chapter 2, page 7)

Her mother is impetuous and self-centred but Elizabeth sweetly reminds her how the introduction to their new neighbours may be made, maintaining all 'civility' (an important word indicating how well a person may be judged in and by their own society).

A lively, playful disposition

A great deal will always be revealed once characters are placed into a social setting. These settings punctuate the story, the first being the public ball at Meryton. Here Elizabeth reacts to Darcy's slight by mocking him, though Austen chooses to use her authorial voice to summarise what Elizabeth *does* rather than reporting the words she says. What she *feels* about the man or his remark is not explicitly stated.

Austen makes us aware of Elizabeth's attractive qualities by analysing Darcy's feelings about her:

…no sooner had he made it clear to himself and his friends that she had hardly a good feature in her face, than he began to find it was rendered uncommonly intelligent by the beautiful expression of her dark eyes…

(Chapter 6, page 20)

Confident in any company

At Netherfield, Elizabeth succeeds in standing up to the unpleasant and ill-mannered comments of Caroline Bingley. In conversation with Darcy she shows she can more than hold her own both in terms of subject matter and of wit (her father's education has worked well).

Text focus

Read Chapter 10, pages 42–43 from '…Elizabeth could not help observing…' to 'He really believed…he should be in some danger.'

● Think about what attracts Darcy to Elizabeth — her wit, her quickness, the absence of the fawning flirtation that Caroline Bingley goes in for.

● Consider also the barriers between them — her prejudice against him, and his haughty attitude towards her family. Each has a long way to go and a great deal to learn before they are ready to be together.

As the story advances we see Elizabeth's good qualities develop. She is caring and loyal and guards her sister, Jane, as far as she can from hurt, as her mother should but does not. She is generally perceptive and a good judge of character, demonstrated by her reaction to Collins' proposal. We do see the usually wise Elizabeth fooled by the superficial 'most gentle-manlike appearance' of handsome, charming Wickham. Flattered by the way he singles her out for attention, her prejudice (and indeed pride) completely contrast with her reaction to Darcy.

She learns more of the Darcy family when she meets, and stands up to, his arrogant aunt Lady Catherine de Bourgh. She is horrified when Darcy makes a proud and reluctant proposal of marriage.

Key quotation

'I might as well inquire,' replied she, 'why with so evident a design of offending and insulting me, you chose to tell me that you liked me against your will, against your reason, and even against your character? Was not this some excuse for incivility, if I *was* uncivil?...'

Elizabeth rejects Darcy's offer of marriage (Chapter 34, page 149)

Able to admit she was wrong

Through reflection, however, she realises how badly she has misjudged his character, especially when she visits Pemberley. The house is the man and she begins to fall in love. She learns that she has jumped to conclusions and that her intelligence does not make her immune to mistakes.

Ultimately we see her grow up. By the end, her pride has been challenged and her prejudice eliminated by learning the truth about the man she loves. Their relationship has made a better human being out of each of them, a fundamental requirement of a good pairing in Austen's judgement. They marry. Elizabeth is rewarded with the love of a very rich man and a wonderful home, but equally she shares the good fortune and her good influence with those around her. The novel does not end at the altar; the final chapter shows how her generosity benefits Georgiana Darcy, the Wickhams and the Gardiners.

TopFoto

Darcy (Matthew Macfadyen) and Elizabeth (Keira Knightley) in the 2005 film

Fitzwilliam Darcy

- is a rich gentleman
- is a serious, proud man
- is intelligent and well educated
- turns out to be morally impeccable and generous

The hero of the novel is harder to get to know than its heroine. This is because Austen gives her authorial point of view to help us judge Elizabeth far more frequently than she does for Darcy. Almost all we learn of him at the outset is through the eyes and judgements of other characters. These judgements are full of contradictions, which readers have to find their own way through. He is introduced in a social setting, at the public ball in Meryton and has all the qualities to make him a hero.

Insufferably proud?

However, Darcy's rejection of the company of the locals immediately makes him a source of annoyance to more than Elizabeth, whose first impression of him is of his pride: he hurts her feelings by refusing to dance with her. (For a full discussion on pride see *Themes*, page 53.) Austen uses her authorial voice to sum up Elizabeth's judgements on the Bingleys, but on Darcy she gives the judgement passed by the characters at the ball:

> ...he was looked at with great admiration for about half the evening, till his manners gave a disgust which turned the tide of his popularity; for he was discovered to be proud...
>
> (Chapter 3, page 10)

From a thoughtful reader's point of view this is not entirely snobbery: he has a right to be distant in a difficult situation but not to make the ungentlemanly remark that upsets Elizabeth.

It soon becomes obvious that he has noticed Elizabeth and finds her attractive, but she continues to judge him harshly because of his initial rejection. Conversation between the two during Elizabeth's stay at Netherfield shows them to be worthy opponents in cut and thrust exchanges of views.

He does not, however, act on his growing feelings, having been exposed to the behaviour of her mother and sisters, particularly at a more formal social gathering, the Netherfield ball.

Text **focus**

Chapter 18 is an important turning point in the novel. The uncouth behaviour of the Bennet family convinces Darcy he needs to separate Bingley from Jane. It also accentuates the social gulf between him and Elizabeth. Read Chapter 18, pages 80–83.

Note how embarrassing Mrs Bennet is, boasting about Jane's chances of marrying Bingley and outstaying her welcome; Mary for her affected piano playing; Mr Bennet by his cruel sarcasm in stopping her; Lydia with her prattle and yawns; Mr Collins by his presumptuous introduction of himself to Mr Darcy and his sycophantic chatter about Lady Catherine de Bourgh.

By comparison with Bingley, Darcy initially seems mean-spirited, though his qualities as a loyal friend begin to show. It becomes clear from his behaviour throughout the novel that Darcy is a close friend of Bingley, which demonstrates his lack of snobbery (Bingley does not come from a landed family — he rents Netherfield). It also becomes clear from his behaviour and letter to Elizabeth that Darcy is guiding his friend in the ways of living as a gentleman and looking out for his interests with loyalty and selflessness.

Darcy's interference in the developing affection between Bingley and Jane is understandable (he is protecting his friend from hurt) though from Elizabeth's initial point of view it looks like cruelty. However, even though he succeeds in keeping his easy-going friend away from the danger of an unsuitable match, he is unable to save himself. His feelings overwhelm his judgement (it is easy to believe that he has never felt so strongly for anyone) and he proposes to Elizabeth (see *Plot and structure*, page 20). His behaviour causes Elizabeth to judge him as ill-mannered, patronising and proudly self–assured. Darcy is not expecting her refusal. He considers himself way beyond the expectations of a girl of Elizabeth's social standing.

Able to admit he was wrong

Elizabeth's rejection is a turning point for Darcy. Her words, especially the accusation that he has not behaved as a gentleman, disturb him greatly. The letter of explanation he writes almost immediately is the reader's first real insight into Darcy's motives (see *Plot and structure*, pages 20–21). He is now at pains to gain Elizabeth's good opinion and explains in detail

why he thought it best to remove Bingley and exactly what Wickham has done to lose his favour. He includes private information about his sister that could be damaging to his reputation if Elizabeth makes it public. The letter demonstrates his integrity, his concern for others close to him and his trust of Elizabeth.

The reader's attitude softens, knowing what it must have cost Darcy to write of such experiences. It takes Elizabeth a little more time to reflect on the information he gives her but eventually she moves from total disbelief to a new understanding of both Darcy and herself.

A liberal gentleman

At Pemberley the true Darcy is revealed (see *Plot and structure*, page 22): the honest comments of his housekeeper and the reflection of the man given by his house and estate complete the reversal of Elizabeth's judgement of him and confirm for the reader what she or he suspected from the start.

Darcy's treatment of the Gardiners is now all civility, despite their social inferiority. The reader sees by his behaviour that his disdain of other members of the Bennet family was grounded on judgement rather than snobbery. Despite his presumed judgement of her actions, he rescues Lydia from shame by paying off Wickham's debts and bribing him to marry her, thus cementing Elizabeth's love for him.

His second proposal to Elizabeth is followed by a conversation between the two which shows Darcy's journey towards self-knowledge (see *Plot and Structure*, page 26). He follows social form by asking her father's permission to marry his daughter and tolerates her mother's reaction to the news. Her good influence on him is promised to continue into their marriage: at the end of the novel we see she was right about their partnership.

Darcy's tolerance and social ease is greatly enhanced by Elizabeth's teasing and 'sportive manner'.

Key quotation

'He is the best landlord, and the best master…There is not one of his tenants or servants but what will give him a good name. Some people call him proud, but I am sure I never saw anything of it.'

Mrs Reynolds of Mr Darcy (Chapter 43, page 190-91)

Key quotation

…by her ease and liveliness, his mind might have been softened, his manners improved…
(Chapter 50, page 239)

Jane Bennet

- is beautiful
- is kind and thinks the best of everyone
- is reliable, discreet and loyal
- is lady-like
- has self-control

Grade *booster*

All the Bennet sisters serve in some way as contrasts to Elizabeth, either to highlight her qualities as a heroine, or to illuminate her human failings. Your ability to comment on the author's use of characterisation, rather than simply discussing characters as if they were real people, will lead to top-grade evaluation.

Jane Bennet (centre, Rosamund Pike) in the 2005 film

Jane, the elder sister, is recognised as the neighbourhood beauty. She is more conventionally attractive, more compliant and less challenging than Elizabeth and therefore at first more like the 'heroine' as these are qualities that men are assumed to value. We are introduced to her by her mother's conversation (Elizabeth is '...not half so handsome as Jane...', page 6). The others all have their opinions about their new neighbour, but the first time Jane contributes to any conversation is after she has caught Bingley's eye and danced with him at the Meryton ball. She is far less willing to be censorious of their new neighbours than her sister. The reader has to concur with Caroline Bingley's judgement of her as 'a sweet girl' (page 16).

In social situations Jane says little: she accepts invitations to dance, she smiles and makes herself pleasant company and she wins affection from all, unlike her more opinionated sister. She is befriended by Caroline Bingley and becomes a welcome visitor at Netherfield. When she takes to bed with a cold, little is heard of her although the Bingleys take care of her and Mr Bingley does not want her to leave.

Jane's intimate conversations with Elizabeth provide a moderating influence on Elizabeth's judgements, for Jane always sees the best in anybody or any situation.

- She defends Darcy against accusations of being disagreeable (Chapter 5).
- She wishes Charlotte happiness in her marriage with Collins (Chapter 24).

> ### Key quotation
>
> '...You never see a fault in anybody. All the world are good and agreeable in your eyes. I never heard you speak ill of a human being in my life.'
>
> Elizabeth of Jane
> (Chapter 4, page 14)

- At different times in the novel, she defends Darcy against Wickham's accusation of bad treatment (Chapter 17), then defends Wickham when the situation is reversed.

At times Jane is naive, but she is not a weak character.

When her hopes of Bingley are dashed by his sudden departure, Jane's ability to suffer in silence becomes her most obvious characteristic. In fact, it is her capacity for concealing strong feelings that lies at the root of Darcy's doubts of her affection for Bingley. Over months, Austen shows the reader that it is her way of coping with separation. She says little, except to Elizabeth, despite her mother's constant talk of his leaving. She writes to Caroline, refusing to believe that she had anything to do with Bingley's change of heart. Even when she stays in London and is rudely ignored by the Bingley sisters, she refuses to see any bad in them and finds reasons for their failure to call on her. The most condemnation she ever shows is in the letter she sends to Elizabeth in Chapter 26 (pages 116–17) and even here she talks of feeling 'pity' and not wishing to 'judge harshly'.

She is rewarded for her goodness by the love of the man she has waited for. Once Darcy is assured that her affection is real, Bingley is encouraged to pursue his suit and they are happily engaged. Mr Bennet shows some insight into his daughter's gentle and generous character when he gives his blessing to the match.

Charles Bingley

- is handsome, rich and charming
- is good-humoured and easy-going
- is kind, but not particularly clever

Grade *booster*

Just as Jane serves a purpose as a contrast with Elizabeth, so Bingley serves a purpose as a contrast to Darcy. Once again, your ability to comment on the author's use of characterisation, rather than simply discussing characters as if they were real people, will lead to top-grade evaluation.

First impressions of him make him seem like the hero of the novel. The narrative begins with a reference to his eligibility as a husband when his plans to rent Netherfield become known. Bingley's looks and sociability make him a favourite at his first social gathering at the Meryton ball. He dances every dance and promises to hold a ball in his new home. He has none of Darcy's intolerance of others.

In conversation he is pleasant and, like Jane, is inclined to see the good in everyone. His attraction to her is also immediate: she is '...the most beautiful creature I ever beheld!' (page 11).

Bingley is rich (£5,000 a year) but his social status is not as great as Darcy's. His father has made money through trade, enough to buy his children an entrance into society. However, they do not have the background of property and land ownership of the upper classes, as does Darcy's family. They are what we might now call *nouveau riche*. Bingley's simple goodness is demonstrated by the way he openly shows his preference for Jane's company. When she becomes ill at Netherfield he is most concerned for her welfare. Elizabeth's arrival there gives more opportunities to study him in conversation with Darcy. He admits to being easily influenced and to disliking arguments in Chapter 10. He is not clever enough to take part in or even enjoy the verbal sparring of Darcy and Elizabeth. He also admits to not being much of a reader or a writer of letters.

He says he is impulsive and his leaving for London so soon after the Netherfield ball reflects this. It is only later that Elizabeth discovers that Darcy has persuaded him that Jane is not the one for him, not simply because of her unsuitable family, which would hardly bother Bingley, but because she has no real feelings for him. This aspect of his behaviour reflects Bingley's compliant nature.

When Bingley discovers that Jane's stay in London was concealed from him he has the spirit to be angry but he is not a man to bear a grudge. He returns to Netherfield and resumes his courtship, charming even the sarcastic Mr Bennet. Darcy watches and, once convinced that Jane returns Bingley's love, gives his approval to the ever-compliant Bingley and prompts the proposal in Chapter 55.

As a couple, Bingley and Jane suit each other well. However, they have much to be grateful for in the continued love and guidance they will receive, for they do not possess the Darcys' capacity for mutual improvement.

> **Pause for thought**
>
> Is it possible to be too nice? Consider that Jane and Bingley both nearly lose a chance of love by putting others first and not always asserting their own will. Do you like them? Would you rather have Jane and Bingley, or Elizabeth and Darcy as friends? Or as a husband, or wife?

The other Bennet sisters

The younger three daughters are less rounded as characters. They are also a contrast to Elizabeth, presented almost as caricatures of female failings rather than as real people.

Mary

Third in terms of age, she is a parody of the idea of an accomplished woman. She is plain and has compensated by bettering herself. Her father introduces her in conversation: '…you are a young lady of deep reflection…and read great books and make extracts' (page 8). When she gives opinions they frequently sound pompous and give the impression that they derive more from her reading than any understanding of the world. Her character contrasts with Elizabeth's, whose comments reflect a sharp intellect and perceptive understanding of the people around her.

Mary is frequently absent from the social occasions that occupy her sisters' time, preferring to read. However, there is one occasion where, by her actions, she contributes to Elizabeth's embarrassment about her family: at the Netherfield ball. Despite Elizabeth's best attempts to deter her, Mary accepts an invitation to sing to the assembled guests. Elizabeth's 'agonies' are shared with the reader through authorial comment: 'Mary's powers were by no means fitted for such a display; her voice was weak, and her manner affected' (page 81). Elizabeth's embarrassment is compounded when Mr Bennet brings the recital to a halt. Mary then slips back into the shadows until the close of the novel where we learn that she benefits from the absence of her sisters as this requires her to spend more of her time socialising with her mother and less time reading and reflecting.

Text focus

Read Chapter 39, pages 170–71 from "'…I do not think it is very pretty…'" to "'How nicely we are crammed in,' cried Lydia.'

Note how Lydia's thoughtless extravagance is emphasised as she shows her older sisters the bonnet she has bought, which she plans to remodel. In fact, the extent of their purchases is a source of some humour for the reader as the girls struggle to fit everything into the coach.

Catherine and Lydia

The younger daughters are almost indistinguishable for the first half of the novel. They are, as their father describes them, 'silly and ignorant', stereotypes at the opposite end of the spectrum from Mary: empty-headed girls, obsessed with shopping, clothes, parties, gossip and flirting with young men. They are their mother's daughters and on many occasions she encourages their frivolous behaviour. They are uneducated, sometimes vulgar and often a source of shame to Elizabeth.

Lydia is brought to the fore when Jane and Elizabeth return from Hunsford. She and Kitty have been allowed to bring the family carriage, unaccompanied, to meet their sisters en route back from London.

Lydia's conversation is unendingly about the officers, particularly Wickham. She becomes a means for Austen to demonstrate how inadequate the Bennets have been as parents. Still not quite 16, Lydia wishes to follow the regiment to Brighton and her mother encourages her—indeed she would like to go with her. Despite Elizabeth's warnings about possible dangers, her father also fails to act responsibly, almost not caring what consequences could follow: '…she cannot grow many degrees worse, without authorising us to lock her up for the rest of her life' (page 180).

The worst does happen: Lydia's flirtations end in elopement with Wickham. This could have destroyed the Bennet family's reputation and any hopes of good marriages for her sisters. Lydia, however, shows by her actions and conversation that she has no shame: she shows off her wedding ring to passing acquaintances, recommends that her sisters follow her example of finding husbands in Brighton and flaunts her feckless husband and married status. She is summed up by an authorial comment as '…untamed, unabashed, wild, noisy, and fearless' (page 241).

Mr and Mrs Bennet

They are an ill-matched couple and the faults of each are exaggerated for humorous effect.

Mr Bennet

Mr Bennet is clever, but has been made cynical by the disappointments of his marriage. He married a silly woman who was beneath his station and now regrets the decision. He spends most of his time hidden away from his women in the library. His cynical commentary on events can be a source of great amusement, particularly when he comments sarcastically on characters like Mr Collins. He is respectful of his two elder daughters, especially Elizabeth who has inherited his incisive wit. Towards the younger daughters, however, he has simply been neglectful, leaving them to their mother and finding their foolishness either a source of irritation or amusement. On several occasions he reflects on his failure to act as he should have done as a wise spouse and father, most notably after Lydia's elopement. However, as a two-dimensional character, he is not going to change. His final remark about admiring all his sons-in-law, though 'Wickham, perhaps, is my favourite…' (page 292), shows he is still the detached, cynical observer of fools that he was at the start of the story.

Mrs Bennet

Mrs Bennet is presented as a woman of little understanding and inferior background, superficial, frivolous and extravagant like her younger

daughters. In her youth she had good looks and good humour, like her daughter Lydia. These qualities have both faded. Failure to produce a son to inherit the estate has left her with little else than the wish to see her daughters married and independent of the consequences of entailment.

She is a caricature of 'ill-breeding': she speaks too loudly and of the most inappropriate or nonsensical things, contradicting herself from one sentence to the next. She is an embarrassment to her daughters in company, notably at the Netherfield ball, where her loud comments about Jane's hopes of marrying Bingley cause Darcy to remove him. She is as selfish as a child and when things do not go the way she wants she falls ill with 'nerves'.

Her husband takes delight in mockery of her. Her failings and 'low connections' are, ironically, the biggest obstacle to what she most wants: marriage for her daughters (see also the Bennets as parents in *Themes*, pages 49–50).

(see also the Bennets as parents in *Themes*, pages 49–50).

Grade *booster*

All novels in the romance genre include a love rival (or two) for the heroine's affections. These rivals turn out to be unsuitable as husbands for a range of reasons. Understanding of literary heritage is an A-grade quality — and this kind of detail demonstrates that you do understand.

Mr Collins, played by Tom Hollander in the 2005 film

Elizabeth's other suitors

Mr Collins

Mr Collins is a truly comic character, a fool made almost grotesque by exaggeration. The presentation of his character goes beyond caricature to satire. He is the nearest male relative to Mr Bennet and thus the heir to Longbourn. His character, from the moment he introduces himself in his letter to Mr Bennet, is shown to be a strange mix of pompous self-importance and cringing deference to his social superiors. His obsequious admiration for Lady Catherine and all she does makes him blind to what she really is: an overbearing busybody. His total lack of self-knowledge and any kind of self-awareness leads him to behave in a manner that embarrasses those around him. Of this he is totally oblivious.

His proposal to Elizabeth reveals him to be devoid of any empathy or understanding of any other point of view than his own. He is hurt when she refuses him as he is unable to comprehend what he has done to deserve rejection. His feelings seem to have limited intensity as he moves almost immediately on to Charlotte Lucas, betraying no awareness at all of how absurd this makes him look.

Working Title/The Kobal Collection

Text *focus*

The irony of Mr Collins' character is that, as a clergyman, he should be humble, tolerant, forgiving, generous and spiritual. He shows himself again and again to be the opposite.

Read part of his letter to Mr Bennet and Mr Bennet's reaction, Chapter 57, page 280 from 'I am truly rejoiced…' to '"…much as I value the impudence and hypocrisy of my son-in-law."'

Notice his extremely unforgiving condemnation of Lydia's behaviour. What is revealed about his character? Think about how this contributes to the amusement of Mr Bennet.

Once home with his new bride, the quality he most exhibits is materialism, both in his attitude to his own 'humble abode' and even more so when he has the opportunity to show off the expensive splendours of Lady Catherine's property. His admiration of cost and quantity disclose a complete lack of taste or discernment.

Mr George Wickham

Mr George Wickham's characterisation contrasts with that of Mr Collins. He is not a comic suitor. At first Austen presents him as competition for Darcy. He seems good-looking, charming, easy company as he singles out Elizabeth for his attentions, taking her into his confidence with the story of how Darcy denied him the promise of a career in the church.

Mrs Gardiner observes the two of them together and warns Elizabeth not to become too involved with Wickham although her warning is about his financial status rather than his character. She is right to be cautious however, because the next we hear of Wickham is that he has transferred his interest to a rich heiress, Miss King.

This is when the truth begins to surface. Elizabeth criticises Darcy's treatment of Wickham when she rejects his proposal. Darcy's response is to reveal the reasons Wickham lost the promised inheritance: he has chosen '…a life of idleness and dissipation' (page 157) rather than a career in the church; he has wasted the money Darcy gave him instead of the promised living and failed to succeed in his second choice of employment, law; he has attempted to elope with Georgiana Darcy to get his hands on her fortune.

Thwarted, he tries his hand at a military career, which comes to a dishonourable conclusion when he succeeds in eloping with Lydia, leaving behind him a muddle of unpaid gambling debts both in Meryton and Brighton.

Pause for thought

Wickham is not a comic character: he is a villain against whom the hero may be judged. How many of Darcy's virtues, such as his morally unimpeachable character, his honesty, his loyalty, his integrity are all the more striking by comparison with George Wickham?

Minor characters

Any novel as long and complex as *Pride and Prejudice* includes a variety of minor and less rounded characters who may contribute to development of plot or themes or simply serve as contrasts to the main characters in the text.

Colonel Fitzwilliam Darcy

- only appears in the book for eight chapters, but is important as a third love rival to the hero
- is Darcy's cousin, and a total contrast to him: agreeable company, intelligent, polite and an entertaining conversationalist
- allows Elizabeth's liveliness and humour to show to best advantage in front of his quieter cousin
- contributes to the theme of money and marriage: a younger son with no hopes of inheriting a fortune, he will have to ensure that he considers money when choosing a wife
- reveals to Elizabeth that Darcy saved his friend, Bingley, from '...the inconveniences of a most imprudent marriage' (page 145) just before, with unfortunate timing, Darcy proposes marriage to her

Mrs Bennet's family

Mrs Philips

- is very like her sister: shallow, frivolous, extravagant and unable to conduct herself properly in polite society
- is fond of company and gossip, with little awareness of propriety; one of the Bennet family connections Darcy finds 'objectionable'.
- is less a source of humour than of amazed embarrassment from any reader who has empathy with Elizabeth's feelings

Mr and Mrs Gardiner

- Mrs Bennet's brother, a total contrast to her: he and his wife are presented as rounded characters, educated and cultured
- Mrs Gardiner grew up in Derbyshire, so suggests visiting Pemberley where they are made welcome by Darcy and conduct themselves faultlessly
- their intelligence and manners are evident despite their lower social class
- contribute to the theme of parenthood and family relationships (see *Themes*, pages 50–51)

Grade *booster*

Mrs Philips represents the unsuitable family connections that act as a barrier to marriage into Darcy's social circles. The Gardiners are a reminder that goodness and civility are not the exclusive birthright of the upper classes. Once again, commenting on the author's use of characterisation, rather than simply discussing characters as if they were real people, will lead to top grade evaluation.

The Bingley sisters

- Miss Caroline Bingley and Mrs Louisa Hurst provide a double act of stereotypical female behaviour
- are untrustworthy, ill-mannered snobs
- are not well educated

The Bingley sisters, by the contrast in their behaviour, serve to emphasise Elizabeth and Jane's positive qualities. Although they are ladies of fashion and position, they are dislikeable characters with negative qualities.

Georgiana Darcy

- by contrast with the Bingley sisters, Georgiana is a real lady
- she reflects positively on her brother to whom she owes gratitude
- a contrast with Lydia, sharing the experience of being ensnared by Wickham, but saved by a caring, competent family, unlike the ineffective Bennets
- shown as requiring the guidance both of her older brother and his chosen wife, whom she grows to love and respect

Charlotte Lucas

- an intimate friend of Elizabeth's, intelligent, sensible and, at 27 years old, mature and level-headed
- she loses some of the reader's sympathy when she marries the ridiculous Mr Collins
- justifies her decision with reasonable arguments about her expectations: rather than being 'an old maid' and a financial burden on her brothers, she takes what comfort she can from a loveless marriage.
- contributes to the theme of marriage (see *Themes* page 47)

Lady Catherine de Bourgh and her daughter, Anne

- Lady Catherine is another great comic creation
- with rank and status superior to most other characters, she has an exaggerated certainty of her own importance
- Mr Collins' awe of her superiority is a source of humour
- her estate at Rosings satirises a fashion for modernising and 'improving' great houses, a contrast with the real beauty of Pemberley (see discussion in *Plot and structure*, page 22).

- plays an important role in advancing the plot when she instructs Elizabeth not to marry Darcy (Chapter 56), leading Elizabeth to wonder whether such a proposal might happen and to dismiss her arguments against it
- Anne is the heiress to Rosings and her mother hopes she will marry Darcy. Anne could not be more of a contrast to her mother, with nothing to say for herself at all
- her only function is to be the peg on which her mother's fantasies and dreams are hung; Elizabeth describes her as '... sickly and cross...' (page 125)

Grade *focus*

How will you be assessed on character-based questions?

Grade	Typical features	At the top end
G–E	Candidates tend to discuss characters as if they are real people. Understanding will be partial and only generalised reference will be made to evidence from the text. There will be little demonstration of alternative interpretations of evidence.	Textual evidence will be used to support clear points, however, interpretation will be simple and straightforward, so aspects of concealed meaning, such as irony or deception are likely to be missed.
D–C	At the top end of the foundation tier, lower end of the higher tier, middle range candidates will select evidence from the text and be able to discuss qualities of character in much more detail.	Top C grade: beginnings of understanding of subtext will be in evidence.
B–A*	In this range of the higher tier paper, there will be more perceptive response to hidden meaning and an ability to grasp irony and alternative readings. Characters will be seen to represent themes and ideas as well as being believable creations.	Evidence will be carefully selected and thoughtfully evaluated. Perceptive analysis and overview of the text typify A grade discussion of characters.

Review your learning

(Answers are given on page 91)

1. Remind yourself of three ways in which Austen reveals characters to her readers.
2. What are the names of the three younger Bennet sisters, and what main purpose do they have in the novel?
3. Which two characters are exaggerated caricatures and what is their impact on the reader?
4. Who do the following phrases describe?
   a '...a sweet girl...'
   b 'fine, tall person, handsome features, noble mien'
   c 'rendered uncommonly intelligent by the beautiful expression in her dark eyes'
   d 'untamed, unabashed, wild, noisy, and fearless'
   e '...sickly and cross...'
5. Who makes the following statements and to whom? What in your opinion does each statement reveal about the speaker?
   a 'You will have a charming mother-in-law, indeed'
   b '...You have delighted us long enough.'
   c '...If I had ever learnt, I should have been a great proficient. And so would Anne...'
   d '...how rich and great you will be! What pin money, what jewels, what carriages you will have!'
   e '...By you I was properly humbled....'

More interactive questions and answers online.

Themes

- What is a theme?
- What are the main themes in *Pride and Prejudice*?
- How do these themes relate to each other?
- How do these themes relate to the characters?
- How will work on themes be assessed?

A theme in a novel is an idea or group of related ideas that the author explores. There is no absolutely correct way to define the themes in a novel, and in any interpretation of literary themes there is bound to be some overlap. Here is a suggested list of themes in *Pride and Prejudice*.

- money and marriage
- parenthood and family life
- love and friendship
- pride and prejudice
- appearance and reality
- social and moral codes

Money and marriage

Pride and Prejudice begins with one of the most famous opening sentences of any novel:

> It is a truth universally acknowledged, that a single man in possession of a good fortune, must be in want of a wife.

Pause for thought

It sounds as though Austen is about to pronounce some great moral insight such as the right to the 'pursuit of happiness' promised in the American Declaration of Independence (1776), which the wording here reflects. What does this sentence mean to you, and why?

The unbreakable link between money and marriage is established right at the beginning. In the context of the novel, love alone cannot be a solid basis for any middle- or upper-class marriage. The fortunes of each of the couple would always have to be an early consideration. However, Austen shows us how education, or the lack of it, can also influence the 'worth' of a character as a potential marriage partner. This theme is prominent in the plot events of the novel, see especially Sections 3 (pages 17–18) and 4 (pages 18–20).

In the book Austen shows four weddings where money plays contrasting levels of importance in making the marriage.

- the Collins
- the Wickhams
- the Bingleys
- the Darcys

The Collinses

The first marriage made is that of Charlotte Lucas to Mr Collins. She marries for financial security. Bear in mind that as well as his comfortable living as a clergyman, he will one day inherit Mr Bennet's estate at Longbourn. At her advanced age of 27, this could well be the only proposal she will ever receive. Charlotte has no personal fortune, but, being the daughter of a knight, she is a good enough social catch for Collins, who is a snob.

There are two things to consider: Charlotte does not seem to expect the relationship of marriage to make her happy, though her status as a married woman, her own home, and the promise of motherhood and a family life attract her. Also, think what her decision to accept Mr Collins says about concern for her 'best' friend Elizabeth, whose cast-off suitor she accepts, and whose home will one day become hers. In the long term, Charlotte's happiness can only be partial. She is an intelligent woman who certainly has little hope of joy from the company of her foolish husband.

> **Key quotation**
>
> '...I am not romantic, you know; I never was. I ask only a comfortable home; and considering Mr. Collins's character, connections, and situation in life, I am convinced that my chance of happiness with him is as fair as most people can boast on entering the marriage state.'
>
> Charlotte defends her choice to Elizabeth (Chapter 22, pages 100–01)

The Wickhams

Second, Wickham and Lydia marry. Their approach to marriage is a complete contrast to Charlotte's. There is no prudence or weighing up of pros and cons: they elope (causing family scandal) to London, caught up in their physical attraction to each other. You will notice that this is about the closest Austen comes to relating marriage to sex. Only family interference makes things right for this marriage. First Darcy and then Lydia's uncle intervene (Chapter 52). In effect they pay Wickham to marry Lydia, ensuring a respectable outcome to the relationship.

In the long term, this marriage too will end unhappily. The poor role model of Lydia's parents shows how marriage based on physical attraction, where the couple have very little in common and where their educational levels are so ill-matched, will end with little joy in companionship once their youth and looks have gone.

There will be a level of resentment too: Wickham hoped to make his fortune through a financially advantageous marriage. He tried for Georgiana Darcy and then Miss King. He will be a poor husband, in both senses of the word: hopeless with money and a womaniser as well. Poor Lydia.

> **Key quotation**
>
> ...such an income as theirs, under the direction of two persons so extravagant in their wants, and heedless of the future, must be very insufficient to their support...
>
> (Chapter 61, page 298)

Text *focus*

Read Chapter 55, page 268. Consider the conversation that follows when newly engaged Jane talks to her parents about prospects in this marriage. It takes us back to the opening of the novel: there is more conversation about finance, appearances and material things than happiness. Remind yourself that Mrs Bennet would have had Bingley as a son-in-law just for his money (so that her daughter would not be reliant on the charity of others if her father was to die). Status is important too: his status and the status of being a married woman for Jane.

The Bingleys

Jane and Bingley have more hopes of a successful future because in their marriage there is a balance between the extremes: they are physically attracted; they take genuine pleasure from each other's company; they are alike in many ways — easy-going and not particularly clever. They also have financial security: Bingley's £5,000 a year.

But this promises to be a marriage offering each of the partners good companionship, even if the outlook seems less than ideal to cynical Mr Bennet (see page 36).

Grade *booster*

Here is another example of an instance where you can demonstrate your top-grade ability to comment on social and historical context. Both money and property indicated the status of men. Bingley's income is good, but he has no property because his father made his fortune fairly recently. Darcy has twice the income and a 'large estate in Derbyshire'. Many people then lived on a wage of between one or two pounds a week: even Bingley is therefore a millionaire by today's standards. The suggestion that these young men are 'in want of a wife' is ironic, but they are certainly eligible marriage material.

The Darcys

Finally there is the ideal, a marriage which will last, based on love, respect and lengthy consideration rather than short-lived passion, a relationship that has grown and changed the two partners in ways that make them even more compatible and better suited.

Darcy and Elizabeth have it all: he is physically attracted to her right from the start and she grows to feel the same attraction to him. However, there is more substance to this relationship: by virtue of education, they are alike in their interests, tastes and views. They have learnt important lessons about how they relate to others, and are likely to go on doing so. Not only are they good for each other, but also to those around them, for example:

> Kitty...spent the chief of her time with her two elder sisters. In society so superior to what she had generally known, her improvement was great...she became, by proper attention and management, less irritable, less ignorant and less insipid...

(Chapter 61, page 297)

Finally, Darcy is the richest man of the four, so Elizabeth also gains the security of money and a fine house. There remains the downside of her embarrassing relatives, but he has an annoying aunt. However, these burdens are lessened by the provision of a role model for a happy marriage in Elizabeth's Aunt and Uncle Gardiner.

Pause for thought

Romantic love is rarely mentioned in connection with marriage in *Pride and Prejudice* — if anything, it is a subject of suspicion. Look at the conversation between Mrs Gardiner and Elizabeth where they discuss the phrase 'violently in love' (Chapter 25, page 111). Do you agree with Mrs Gardiner's comments? Note, however, that Darcy describes his love for Elizabeth as 'ardent' and Austen uses the phrase 'violently in love' to sum up his feelings.

Parenthood and family relationships

How well or badly does a marriage impact on the upbringing of children? Again, a number of relationships are presented for the reader to consider:

- the Bennets
- the Gardiners
- the Lucases

The Bennets

Working Title/The Kobal Collection

The Bennet family in the 2005 film (*left–right*: Lydia, Mr Bennet, Jane, Mrs Bennet, Catherine, Elizabeth and Mary)

Key quotation

[Elizabeth]...had never felt so strongly as now the disadvantages which must attend the children of so unsuitable a marriage, nor ever been so fully aware of the evils arising from so ill-judged a direction of talents; talents which, rightly used, might at least have preserved the respectability of his daughters...

Elizabeth reflects on her father's failings after Lydia's elopement (Chapter 42, page 183)

Mr and Mrs Bennet's marriage began with the same kind of attraction as that shown between Lydia and Wickham. This has now faded and they have little pleasure in their relationship with each other.

Mrs Bennet brought some money into the marriage: 'Five thousand pounds was settled by marriage articles on Mrs Bennet and the children'

Text focus

Read the opening of Chapter 50, page 236. Consider Mr Bennet's regrets about his failings as a provider for his daughters.

(page 236). However, Mr Bennet has not been prudent with the family finances. He has failed to save enough to ensure a secure future for his daughters after his death, when the estate goes to Mr Collins.

Despite their less than perfect marriage, as parents the Bennets seem to have done quite well in the upbringing of their elder daughters: Jane is a good person and Elizabeth's intellect and wit have been encouraged. However, the impact of a silly, ill-educated mother and a sarcastic father who has retreated impatiently into his library is clear in the younger three. Kitty and Lydia, encouraged by their mother, are silly, obsessed by hats, dancing and young men, while Mary strives to be accomplished without her father's guidance or Elizabeth's intelligence.

A mismatch between their education and, in Mr Bennet's case, a failure to turn intellect into intelligent action, has undermined their effectiveness as parents. (There is further discussion of Mr and Mrs Bennet in *Characterisation*, pages 39–40.)

The Gardiners

Mrs Bennet's brother presents a contrasting representation of family life. Mr Gardiner is of a lower social class — first mentioned and snobbishly dismissed by Caroline Bingley as living '…somewhere near Cheapside' (page 30). However, this family life is presented as one well worthy of emulation. The Gardiners' London address may not have the social status of the Hursts', but their life is comfortable and civilised with visits to the theatre and shopping in the city. As parents, the Gardiners are a success: their '…troop of little boys and girls…' (page 120) are loved and cared for.

In contrast to her husband's sisters, Mrs Gardiner has an intellect which matches her husband's, good manners and good sense '…an amiable, intelligent, elegant woman…' (page 110). We grow to know her better than her husband as she spends time with Elizabeth, warning her to be wary of a relationship with Wickham and offering the distraction of a trip to the north of England when that relationship comes to nothing. She also supports Jane after her disappointment with Bingley. In essence she plays the role of a concerned mother far better than the girls' real one.

Mr Gardiner takes on the fatherly role that should rightly have been Mr Bennet's, dealing with the consequences of Lydia's elopement. At the end of the novel, as good parents to their own children, this couple become role models for, and welcome guests of, the couple at Pemberley.

Key quotation

With the Gardiners they were always on the most intimate terms. Darcy, as well as Elizabeth, really loved them

(Chapter 61, page 299)

The Lucases

The Bennets' neighbours in Longbourn provide another picture of family life. Sir William has a background in trade and has been mayor, which led to his receiving a knighthood. He has spent some of his money on Lucas Lodge and there affects the manners he has learnt at the court of St James's, hugely impressed by anyone whose status he perceives to be higher than his own. His wife, Lady Lucas, is described as '...not too clever to be a valuable neighbour to Mrs Bennet' (page 16).

They have 'several children' (page 16), the oldest being Charlotte who demonstrates cynical views about marriage (see *Money and Marriage*, page 47) and a younger daughter, Maria, whose awe of her social superiors is shown to be like her father's when they visit Lady Catherine in Chapter 29 (pages 126–27).

One of her younger brothers expresses the opinion that if he '...were as rich as Mr Darcy...I should not care how proud I was. I would keep a pack of foxhounds, and drink a bottle of wine every day' (page 18). The Lucas parents seem to provide limited role models for happy family life.

The young couples

Good marriages lead to solid parenting and the reader is invited to speculate about how the quality of the various marriages shown will shape their family life. The Darcys and Bingleys begin to act as parents to Kitty even before they have children of their own. Jane has already had practice with her Gardiner nephews and nieces, '...teaching them, playing with them and loving them' (page 186). Both couples have promise as parents.

The best that can be hoped for the Collinses' children is that they will have a sensible loving mother. The insubstantial basis for the Wickhams' marriage holds out little hope for any children.

Love and friendship

Ideally love and friendship are a part of marriage, but not necessarily so, as the themes above show. Good friendships, like good marriages, lead to the mutual improvement and growth of both parties.

Elizabeth and Jane

Elizabeth and Jane are friends as well as sisters and Elizabeth's ability to give support and guidance compensates for their inadequate parents. All major events in their lives are shared in person or by letter: for example Jane's disappointment when the Bingleys leave Netherfield, and her hurt feelings when she is slighted by Caroline in London. They talk over Darcy's supposed injury to Wickham's prospects and the truth about why Darcy acted as he did. They share the shame and anxiety Lydia causes and finally take joy from each other's happiness at the conclusion of the

novel, though not before Jane has assured herself that Elizabeth is not planning to '…marry without affection' (page 288). Jane's benevolence and Elizabeth's intelligence are the basis for life-long friendship with a positive impact on both.

Charlotte and Elizabeth

Charlotte and Elizabeth have a close friendship that continues despite Charlotte's unpromising marriage. She is introduced as being 'a sensible, intelligent young woman' (page 16) and there are certainly occasions where her opinions prove to be right in the long term. She advises Elizabeth that Darcy's stand-offish behaviour at the Meryton ball may have been misinterpreted. She warns her that Jane may be limiting her chances of romance with Bingley by not making her feelings more obvious — the very reason Darcy decides to separate them.

Elizabeth's reservations about Charlotte's marriage to Collins make her question whether they will ever share confidences in the same way they had been used to. However, they remain friends. Charlotte is the first person to suspect that Darcy might be in love with Elizabeth (Chapter 32) and certainly Elizabeth's sympathy for Charlotte's situation in Hunsford is heartfelt.

Darcy and Bingley

Darcy and Bingley also have a good friendship. Darcy sees Bingley's faults (much as Elizabeth is aware of Jane's and Charlotte's): his trusting nature (he might not realise that Jane could be a fortune hunter, given the general attitude to marriage in Meryton) and his reluctance to argue with or hurt people. He decides to remove Bingley from Jane before any harm is done.

This friendship reveals that Darcy is not a snob: his background and social status are superior to Bingley's (Caroline's lack of manners makes this clear) but this does not hold him back. He and Bingley have qualities which are mutually beneficial and will go on being so throughout life: like Elizabeth, Bingley helps to soften Darcy's seriousness and to encourage his sociability, while Darcy will shape the suggestible Bingley into a country gentleman of his own kind.

Pride and prejudice

As with many of Austen's themes, the idea of opposition and balance is implied here. When you first begin to read, it is easy to think this theme is a simple matter of Darcy being too proud (and having to learn not to be) and Elizabeth being prejudiced against him (and having to learn not to be).

Not so straightforward, however: Darcy is also early on shown to be prejudiced when he claims he will rarely revise negative judgements (remember the novel was originally written with the title of *First Impressions*).

> **Key quotation**
>
> 'I remember hearing you once say, Mr Darcy, that you hardly ever forgave, that your resentment once created was unappeasable. You are very cautious, I suppose, as to its *being created*.'
>
> 'I am,' said he, with a firm voice.
>
> 'And never allow yourself to be blinded by prejudice?'
>
> 'I hope not.'
>
> 'It is particularly incumbent on those who never change their opinion, to be secure of judging properly at first.'
>
> Elizabeth and Darcy (Chapter 18, pages 75–76)

Pride

Elizabeth, too, is proud. She responds to hurt pride in her rejection of Darcy, both at the start of the novel and when he makes his first unwilling and ungracious proposal to her.

Darcy's superior rank gives him reason to be distant in comparatively humble company and this is not simple snobbery. From a thoughtful reader's point of view, as Charlotte reminds us, his 'pride' at Meryton was justified: in a room full of unfamiliar people, socially inferior to him, well knowing that many of those present will see him as a 'good catch' for someone's daughter, a girl of a social class he would judge as unequal to his own.

Darcy puts his manners down to shyness later in the book (page 137), a quality he is shown to share with his younger sister, though he is prepared to admit he has been guilty of thinking '...meanly of all the rest of the world...of their sense and worth compared with my own' (page 284). He tells Elizabeth that her words as she rejected his first proposal set him on the path to remedying that fault of character.

Text focus

Austen offers us an interesting distinction between pride and vanity. At the end of Chapter 5, pages 17–18, Charlotte Lucas speaks sense about Darcy (from 'His pride...does not offend *me*...' to '...he has a *right* to be proud'). Now look at Mary's words (from '...Vanity and pride are different things...' to '...we would have others think of us'). Is Mary for once showing more insight than her clever sister?

Prejudice

Elizabeth's hurt pride leads her into trouble, making her an easy catch for Wickham: his stories of mistreatment by Darcy reflect her bad opinion and fuel her dislike. Conversely, Wickham flatters her pride by singling her out and treating her as special. It is only after she learns the truth about him that she realises that prejudice in his favour prevented her from questioning the appropriateness of his easy intimacy when they hardly knew each other.

Two events undo the damage: first, Elizabeth's angry reaction to Darcy's proposal provokes him to write his letter. This goes a long way towards explaining his actions and allows her to reconsider the defects of character she believed him to have (see *Plot and structure*, pages 20–21 for a full discussion), while he begins to find self-knowledge through the writing of it.

Second, Elizabeth's visit to Pemberley eradicates any lingering feelings of prejudice: seeing Darcy's house explains his discomfort in the parochial world of Meryton, and hearing everyone in his household talk of him with such warmth upends her prejudiced opinions. He, likewise, takes the opportunity to greet her relations with a warmth and civility their social status would not have warranted with no hint of pride or superiority (see *Plot and structure*, pages 22–23)

By the time he proposes and she accepts, each has learnt a valuable lesson in tempering pride and overcoming prejudice: judgements will still be made, for they are both thinking, rational people, but they will see more clearly and jump to conclusions with less haste in their maturity.

Grade *booster*

If you are asked to write about the theme of pride and prejudice, don't focus too narrowly on Elizabeth and Darcy. Think about the other characters in the novel who contribute in a minor way to the theme of pride and prejudice: what could you add about the pride of Sir William Lucas and the lack of personal pride of his daughter, Charlotte? What about the small town prejudices of Mrs Bennet?

Vanity

There are minor characters in the novel held up for comparison with Darcy who illustrate Mary's point (see Text focus, page 53) about the difference between pride and vanity.

Lady Catherine is truly vain, with no real reason. Everything she says shows her self-centred attitude and conviction that she is always right and always better than everybody else. Compare her unwanted advice to her tenants (page 128) with Darcy's genuine concern for their well-being (pages 190–91).

Caroline Bingley is also vain and self-centred. Her snobbery towards Elizabeth and Jane shows her to be less of a genuine lady than she thinks herself.

Mr Collins is vain in thinking that the reflected glory of Lady Catherine's connection with him makes him better than others. It also makes him pompous, self-centred and stupid to a remarkable degree.

Appearance and reality

Austen investigates another opposition linked to the theme of pride and prejudice: how what *appears* to be may be very far from reality. Superficial judgements made by the unthinking crowd are almost always incorrect. The first line in the book ought to make you ask questions as soon as you start reading: would any single rich young man always need a wife? Why should he? Who would benefit more from the arrangement?

Elizabeth and Darcy both make judgements based on superficial appearance, about each other and about those around them. It takes months to put things right, as shown in the discussion of their pride and prejudice above.

All the Bennet family judge Wickham as the splendid young man he appears to be — and all are let down by him.

The underlying idea of balance

Austen is warning us to be wary of hasty and impulsive behaviour based on emotion rather than reflection.

She is arguing against the growing Romantic admiration for spontaneity and emotion (see *Context*, page 9) and shows her readers that a middle way, finding a balance between reason and feeling, head and heart, is the best and most sensible option.

Social and moral codes

Even today, England is a country where social class boundaries are more evident than in other parts of the world, but this was much more so in Austen's time and the theme of social and moral codes reflects the existence of a strict hierarchy. However, the boundaries were blurring between:

- nobility (those with titles, Lords and Dukes), the 'fashionable' class
- gentry (those with land and status)
- the upper middle class (those who had risen in the world through money made in the professions such as law, the military or the church)
- those who had bought their way into the upper middle class with fortunes acquired by recent success in trade and industry, often coupled with buying a gentleman's education for their sons

This list defines the characters Austen writes about. Relationships are bound up with strict codes of etiquette that control all social and moral dealings with each other.

It was a world with rigid routines and rituals of lifestyle: the fashionable class enjoyed summer in the country house, the winter season in London,

visits to spa towns like Bath with entertainment such as theatre and dances, trips to the seaside in the summer (the Prince Regent's fondness for Brighton started this) or trips to the wilds of the north of England or even Scotland.

Going against the rules would lead to criticism or even exclusion from a social group (as would have happened to Georgiana Darcy and Lydia, had their experiences at the hands of Wickham and Mrs Younge ended differently). To an outsider, or to us, separated from this society by 200 years of social change, it looks like a mercenary, snobbish, narrow-minded world of people, obsessed with trivia. To be excluded from this society, however, would have been very serious, cutting off opportunities for a gentleman to advance in the world and for a girl to find a suitable husband to support her.

The word 'civility', which means understanding and applying the rules that bind society together, is a central one in the novel. Elizabeth can throw no greater insult to the well-bred Darcy than to describe his behaviour as 'uncivil' and less than 'gentlemanlike'. (More information relevant to this theme can be found in *Context*, pages 10–12.)

Review your learning

(Answers are given on page 92.)

1. Which five main themes are identified in this guide?
2. Which marriages illustrate the theme of family life?
3. Who is presented as the main example of the theme of appearance and reality?
4. Which theme is most closely associated with the historical context of the novel?
5. Why is the theme of marriage related to money rather than love?
6. Which theme do you consider to be the most important in the novel? Think of at least three reasons for your answer.

More interactive questions and answers online.

Style

- What features does the term 'style' refer to?
- What viewpoint does Austen adopt?
- How is dialogue used to tell the story?
- Why are so many letters included in the novel?
- What is significant about Austen's use of description and settings?

Anyone who has read *Pride and Prejudice,* or seen one of the adaptations of the book, will be able to retell the story. However, this is a low-level skill and will gain few marks. Many exam questions ask you to comment on characters or themes, requiring you to use knowledge of the novel to provide evidence for your analysis.

When you write about style, you are showing that you understand that the author of a novel has numerous choices. Your job as a literary critic — because that is what you are when you write your exam essay — is to identify what choices Austen has made and to assess how effective they are.

The list below gives some of the main features covered by the word 'style'. Austen has made choices about all of them.

- the **viewpoint** from which the story is told, whether it is third person narrative ('**Elizabeth** passed quietly out of the room' or '**She** turned from the window') or first person narrative ('**I** turned from the window')
- how **dialogue** (conversation) is used to advance the narrative and reveal character
- how **letters** are used to advance the narrative and reveal character
- how **description** of people and settings adds to the story
- how techniques such as **exaggeration**, **caricature**, **irony and satire** add humour to the novel

Viewpoint

The viewpoint of a novel is the position from which the author tells the story. Some novels are told from a **first person** viewpoint, for example this story could have been told from Elizabeth Bennet's viewpoint. That would have made a different story as we would possibly have found out a great deal more about Elizabeth's view of things, but rather less about other characters in the novel.

Instead, Austen tells the story in the **third person**. The author is the **narrator** and the characters are referred to by their names, or as 'he' or 'she'. This allows Austen to tell us her views about all characters and events as the plot unfolds, as well as allowing her to move from one character to another and describe how they see events.

Grade *booster*

Writing about viewpoint in your exam will help you to reach the higher grades. Two useful terms to understand:

- **omniscient narrator** — the story-teller knows everything about everyone in the story and tells the reader the truth
- **unreliable narrator** — the story is communicated using the point of view of a character who may be biased or know only some of the facts

Austen keeps readers on their toes by moving between the two. You will raise your marks if you are able to understand *where* she does this and explain *why*.

Although the story is written in the third person, it is easy to read on a superficial level as the viewpoint identifies and empathises with Elizabeth. She is the main character and much of the time, although not always, experiences are narrated as she sees them.

Text focus

Austen often uses a technique where, although she writes about her characters in the third person, she chooses different viewpoints and perspectives to reveal information that is not known to everyone. Read Chapter 6, pages 20–22 from 'Occupied in observing Mr Bingley's attentions to her sister…' to '…joined eagerly in dancing at one end of the room.' Then read the explanation below.

- You will see that this extract begins by allowing the reader to share a viewpoint not often seen, that of Mr Darcy. The first paragraph tracks the changes in his feelings about Elizabeth, from critical of her looks the first time he sees her, to a realisation that her face: 'was rendered uncommonly intelligent by the beautiful expression of her dark eyes'.
- It goes on to describe the experience as 'mortifying' when he begins to find 'her figure to be light and pleasing' and is attracted by the 'easy playfulness' of her manners.
- This gives the reader insight into Darcy's private thoughts and feelings: no one else knows them, especially not Elizabeth. The paragraph concludes by telling us she was 'perfectly unaware' of this. Here Austen writes as the **omniscient narrator** commenting on a character but then she moves immediately to Elizabeth's personal opinion of Darcy: 'only the man who made himself agreeable nowhere', a biased and **unreliable** opinion.
- An exchange of dialogue follows, then Austen returns to the viewpoint of the omniscient narrator as she compares Elizabeth's singing ('… pleasing, though by no means capital') with that of her sister Mary who plays better but gives less pleasure because she '…had neither genius nor taste'.

As you read, you will notice that chapters frequently open with **narrated information**. The viewpoint can vary as in the extract above. The opening of Chapter 15 (page 57) begins with Austen's **authorial opinion** of Mr Collins' character ('...not a sensible man', '...the self-conceit of a weak head') but then moves at the end of the second paragraph into Collins' own opinion of his 'plan of amends' as 'excessively generous and disinterested'.

Irony

Irony is a feature of style that Austen uses extensively.

A statement is **ironic** if the truth of it is the opposite of the surface appearance. The unreliability of general opinion is a good example of this. Some characters speak ironically by putting forward opinions they do not really hold. Mr Bennet does this regularly.

If Austen puts forward the viewpoint of 'everyone' or 'all the town' has an opinion or judgement, then it will be wrong.

- The novel opens with a famous statement about 'a truth universally acknowledged...' where the 'young man' in question is the last one to be looking for a wife, though those around him may very well be interested in marrying him off.
- In Chapter 3, judgements about Mr Darcy change from his being 'handsomer than Mr Bingley' to 'having a most forbidding, disagreeable countenance' within a single paragraph (page 10) What causes the change?
- On the other hand, in Chapter 18, one of the officers tells Elizabeth that Wickham is 'universally liked' (page 73). She has had her warning.

Dialogue

The **conversational novel** was a recent form that Austen adopted with enthusiasm. In all Austen's novels a great deal of the narrative is developed through conversation and the style of the dialogue is a central method of revealing characters to the reader.

Early in the novel, we learn a great deal about all the characters in Bingley's group at Netherfield through dialogue.

Text focus

Turn to Chapter 11, pages 45–48. First, note how much of what is written in this chapter is dialogue. Now read page 45 in detail from 'Miss Bingley's attention was quite as much engaged...' to the end of the chapter.

- The conversation begins with irony: Caroline Bingley puts down the book she has been pretending to read and, with a yawn, says, 'How much sooner one tires of anything but a book!' She clearly has little interest in hers, but goes on to comment that she would be '...miserable if I have not an excellent library' in her own home. Earlier conversation was about Elizabeth's fondness for reading and Darcy's extensive library at Pemberley. The book Caroline has been pretending to read is the second volume of the one Darcy has chosen, thus two things become clear: the first that she is trying to impress Darcy by imitation and flattery; the second that she is competing for his attention with Elizabeth. She is jealous.
- Conversation moves on to the possibility of a ball at Netherfield. Bingley's comments show him to be practical: he mentions food, invitations and says that Darcy can spend the evening in bed if he doesn't wish to join in. Caroline, to impress Darcy, begins to philosophise that balls would be better if there was '...conversation instead of dancing...'. The unintentional irony of this is picked up by her brother's witty reply that '...it would not be near so much like a ball.'

- Her next move to encourage Darcy to take notice of her is to walk about the room. When that fails, she asks Elizabeth to join her. This does get his attention. He is invited to join them, but his two reasons why they would not wish him to do so show his wit and insight: either 'you have secret affairs to discuss' or 'your figures appear to the greatest advantage in walking'. Caroline says he should be punished for this comment.
- Elizabeth shows a quality we know Darcy admires: her lively mind. She is his equal in sparring with words and she suggests how they should punish him: 'Tease him — laugh at him'. Her judgement of Darcy as proud and serious is at the root of this and the interchange that follows leads to their agreement that all people have weaknesses that are open to ridicule. Darcy's comment that '...pride will always be under good regulation' in a person with '...superiority of mind' provokes a smile from Elizabeth as she sees that as ironic.
- Darcy then shows insight, and respect for Elizabeth's opinion, as he explores his faults. Caroline shows she has not understood the conversation and changes the subject, Bingley has nothing to contribute and Mr Hurst has been asleep, showing that even those who do not speak can reveal some aspect of their character in a sequence of dialogue.

Comic characters

Comic characters reveal themselves to the reader through extensive dialogue. Some characters are exaggerated to the point of **caricature.** Here we see another of Austen's key techniques, as she uses **satire** to bring their faults to the reader's attention. As we laugh at Collins' hypocrisy or Lady Catherine's self-importance, we are also being invited to form opinions about these negative qualities.

Text focus

Read Chapter 14, pages 54–55 (Collins dines at Longbourn) and Chapter 29, pages 128–130 (Lady Catherine entertains at Rosings). What judgements do we make about their characters through the content of their comments and the language they use?

Letters

Letter writing, as *Pride and Prejudice* shows, was a skill that women were encouraged to acquire, especially those who lived quiet lives isolated in the country for large parts of the year. Austen was an enthusiastic correspondent and it is notable that the characters she leads us to admire are all able to construct a good letter (even the men), while the ones who are held up for criticism often fail in this respect as well as others.

Mr Bennet and his daughters read news of Lydia and Wickham in a letter from Edward Gardiner in the 2005 film

The epistolary novel

The epistolary novel, a narrative made up entirely of letters sent between the characters, was a popular genre in Austen's time. *Pride and Prejudice* may have started out in this form as *First Impressions*. Although it is not an epistolary novel, letters do play an important part in the story. Around 30 letters are mentioned as being written or received and of these over ten are included in whole or part in the words of their writer.

Letters serve four major functions for the reader. They may:

1 contain **information** about events and sometimes directly influence plot development
2 allow an author to write from a specific **viewpoint** in the first person (as 'I') thus revealing a great deal about the character of the writer (in a similar way to dialogue) and their feelings about events
3 advance certain **themes** of the novel
4 indicate the **relationship** that exists between the sender and the receiver

Darcy's letters

Darcy is shown to be a keen letter writer when he writes to his sister in Chapter 10 (pages 38–40). In conversation with Caroline Bingley we

learn that he writes regularly, at length and with care. This shows him to advantage and makes Caroline and Charles Bingley seem rather shallow by comparison.

Text **focus**

One of Darcy's letters is presented in its entirety: the letter of explanation he sends to Elizabeth after she rejects his proposal in Chapter 35, page 152 and following. It is lengthy — so long that it is in an 'envelope'. Letters were usually a sheet of paper folded and addressed on the blank side then sealed with sealing wax. The envelope referred to here is a folded sheet of paper enclosing the other two sheets and that was 'likewise full'.

- The first function of this letter is to reveal the character of Darcy to the reader in his own words. Austen rarely writes from his viewpoint, and in dialogue he is not often a major contributor. The letter shows him to be responsible, honest, intelligent and concerned for the welfare of others. He is anxious to explain himself to Elizabeth and answer her criticisms of his character and behaviour. His concern for Bingley's happiness, his respect for his father and care for his sister are all clear. The sincere and thoughtful tone of the letter is as important as its content in underlining the kind of man he is.

- Second, the letter demonstrates his feelings for Elizabeth. He values her sufficiently to excuse his arrogant proposal. He also trusts her enough to reveal potentially damaging information about the relationship of Wickham and his sister. The letter builds more intimacy between them than his proposal of marriage. The letter marks a turning point in the main plot, as it starts the process by which Elizabeth and Darcy begin to change in response to each other, ultimately leading to their marriage.

- Third, there is information that advances the plot: the true story of Wickham's loss of support from Darcy. It also foreshadows Wickham's elopement with Lydia.

- Finally, a theme is brought to the fore: the untrustworthiness of appearance. Wickham is not who he appeared to be and Elizabeth realises that Darcy is not the proud man he has seemed and is worthy of admiration. The letter also reveals Darcy's family background and contributes to the theme of family life as lived by the different characters.

Mrs Gardiner's letters

Mrs Gardiner is also shown to be a regular correspondent. She and Elizabeth write about Jane while she stays in London and share misgivings about Wickham and plans for the trip north. Through Mrs Gardiner's letters the reader knows her to be thoughtful, sensible and concerned for her nieces' wellbeing.

Mr Collins' letters

Mr Collins' letters to Mr Bennet could not be a greater contrast to the serious correspondence above. Two of them are included in their entirety, the first as he introduces himself and announces he is to visit

Text focus

The most important letter Mrs Gardiner sends, again included as a full text in the novel, is the reply to Elizabeth's enquiry as to what Darcy was doing at Lydia's wedding. Read Chapter 52, pages 246–250.

- Much is revealed that affects the plot: Darcy knew where to find the runaways through Mrs Younge, Georgiana's untrustworthy ex-companion; Darcy spent time meeting Wickham; a lot of money changed hands to ensure the pair were married.
- The closeness of Mrs Gardiner's relationship with Elizabeth is stressed: she trusts her to keep this information from her mother and father, she alludes to Darcy's probable motives for helping in such a way, ending with a request to be invited to Pemberley. Her trusted aunt's letter is another point on Elizabeth's journey towards marriage to Darcy.

Pause for thought

Just as dialogue can be a source of humour, so are letters written by comic characters. Here too exaggeration and satire are in evidence.

(pages 51–52), the second after Lydia's elopement (page 227). Both show Collins to be a pompous, priggish man, lacking the logic and self-knowledge to see the contradictions in his own writing. They help to create a caricature of the man and are a source of some sarcastic humour both to the reader and Mr Bennet.

Lydia's letters

Lydia's letters also contain elements of caricature reflecting her failures and follies. When she goes to Brighton, she writes infrequently and briefly to her parents; it later turns out she has been writing in more detail to Kitty, letters said to be 'too full of lines under the words to be made public'. Lydia's extravagant writing style and outrageous comments are a reflection of the silly, unguarded nature of her conversation.

Two complete letters are included, both revealing her thoughtless and self-centred character: her farewell note to Mrs Forster when she elopes from Brighton (page 223), and her congratulations to Elizabeth (page 298).

Description

By comparison with many writers, there is little in the way of physical description of people or places in Austen's novels. We are largely left to imagine for ourselves what characters look like. Remarks from other characters, or the authorial voice, sometimes provide details such as Darcy's height and seriousness, Elizabeth's 'fine eyes' and tanned complexion, Jane's reputation as a beauty, Lydia's being 'tall and well-grown'.

Word pictures instead of imagery

Austen uses little imagery in terms of similes and metaphors, but she does build up 'word pictures' to help readers understand a personality. Her distinctive style allows her to sum up a character in a few well-chosen words:

- She chooses precise adjectives to describe characters' actions and thoughts.
- She emphasises details about a character by saying what they are not, or by contrast with someone else.

Text focus

Read Charlotte's thoughts about her intended husband and consider what you learn about their personalities (Chapter 22, pages 98–99). Now consider how Austen describes Lady Catherine, Colonel Fitzwilliam and Darcy in these two extracts: (1) introduction to Lady Catherine, Chapter 29, page 127 and (2) Darcy and Colonel Fitzwilliam pay their first visit to Hunsford, Chapter 30, page 134.

Settings

Places are important in *Pride and Prejudice*. The action moves from fictional towns and villages (like Meryton and Longbourn) in the real county of Hertfordshire, to real streets in London, to Kent and back into fiction (at Hunsford parsonage and the estate at Rosings). Sometimes names of towns are given simply as blanks, indicating a real town but one the author has chosen not to identify and at other times real places like Brighton and Newcastle are named. When the Gardiners journey to Derbyshire Austen lists the real towns they pass through (Oxford, Blenheim, Warwick, Kenilworth, Birmingham, see page 186) but invents the village of Lambton and Darcy's estate at Pemberley.

It seems that Austen worked with a map to locate her geographical settings much as she worked with a calendar to plot the sequence of events. Even so, like her characters, the appearance of the places is rarely described in any detail, with a few exceptions, for example the parsonage at Hunsford and the grand house at Rosings, which are seen through Mr Collins' admiring descriptions.

Pemberley

The most detailed description of any place is to be found when Elizabeth visits Pemberley. Detailed discussion of the significance of this description is given in *Plot and Structure* (page 22). This, and the use of the seasons as a background for events (see *Plot and structure*, page 26), are the only evidence of symbolism in this novel.

PHILIP ALLAN LITERATURE GUIDE FOR GCSE

Grade *focus*

You are not likely to be asked a question in the exam which focuses only on style. You will, however, gain marks for showing how use of language contributes to the presentation of character or theme.

Grades D–C

At the upper end of the foundation paper candidates will be able to identify some aspects of style. For example, they may be able to comment on how well-chosen adjectives communicate something about a character or a setting. They would be able to show how viewpoint is communicated and how dialogue and letters allow for changes of viewpoint, with suitable examples of evidence selected from the text.

Grades B–A*

The real difference is the appreciation of a variety of features of style for B grade, and increasingly sophisticated evaluation and analysis of textual evidence to reach the highest grades.

Use the sample essays in the next section to see how response to style is assessed by your examiner.

Language

Any novel written more than 200 years ago must present some challenges to the reader because meanings of words change over time. When Austen uses words such as 'gentleman', 'civil', 'liberal', or talks about people passing the evening playing 'lottery', these words are not used in the same sense as we now understand them. Watch out for these words and other examples — find out how meanings for each differ from now and keep notes to remind yourself.

Review your learning

(Answers are given on page 93)

1 What is an epistolary novel, and how is *Pride and Prejudice* influenced by this genre?

2 How is dialogue used to reveal characters to the reader? Which characters do you think have particularly distinctive manners of speaking?

3 Name three techniques used to incorporate humour into the novel.

4 How does Austen change the viewpoint used to communicate the narrative? Explain three techniques she uses to do this.

5 Is symbolism used in *Pride and Prejudice*?

6 What stylistic technique does Austen use instead of imagery?

More interactive questions and answers online.

Tackling the assessments

- **What is an essay?**
- **What are the three main parts of a well-structured essay?**
- **How should you plan and structure your assessment essay?**
- **How should you provide evidence to support your interpretation of the text?**
- **What will turn a C-grade essay into an A*-grade essay?**

You will be assessed on your knowledge of *Pride and Prejudice* in one of two ways:

- by taking a final exam where you will not know in advance what you may be asked to write about
- *or* by completing a controlled assessment, preparing for the task in school before writing your answer over a longer period of time than an exam

Whichever you do, you will be writing an essay. This section gives advice about essay writing, as well as looking at the kinds of tasks you could be asked to complete.

Planning

Whatever the question, your first job is to plan your essay. Some exam questions include a list of three or four bullet-point hints, which provide you with the basis of your plan.

Recognising the type of question

Here is an example of a typical foundation-tier exam question:

> Examine the relationship between Elizabeth and Charlotte in the novel. In your answer, you may consider:
> - Elizabeth's friendship with Charlotte
> - the words and actions of Charlotte
> - the different attitudes of Elizabeth and Charlotte to marriage
>
> You may include other ideas of your own.

Other questions are just a title with no hints for what to include. To answer these you need to break the question down and use your own ideas as the basis for your plan.

Here is an example of a controlled assessment question of the type set by AQA:

> Explore the ways Austen presents family relationships in *Pride and Prejudice*.

Here is an example of a higher-tier exam question:

> How does Austen present the theme of marriage in *Pride and Prejudice*?

Breaking down the question in an exam

If you feel under pressure in an exam, it is tempting to read a question quickly and start writing immediately. Stop! You should read the question carefully, at least twice, and if it is a higher-tier question, you should attempt to break it down into parts to work out exactly what you are being asked to do. This will help to ensure that you answer the question that is being asked and not the one that you think is being asked or for which you have prepared.

Here is a possible breakdown for the question on the theme of marriage. The question gives you little guidance for your planning, so you could break this question down as follows:

- Introduction — briefly — reasons why marriage was a goal for women in Austen's time (less chance of education, financial independence) link with novel's opening sentence. Several marriages, successful and less successful presented in the novel for the reader to consider and judge.
- Three marriages which are questionable, for different reasons: Mr and Mrs Bennet (not well matched, no mutual respect, poor parents as a result); Mr Collins and Charlotte (a loveless marriage for status, money and security, no real pleasure in each other's company); Mr Wickham and Lydia (based on passing physical attraction alone — a little like Lydia's own parents — no financial security).
- Three happy marriages held up in contrast: Mr Bingley (£5,000 a year) and Jane (a genuine love match between well-suited partners but they may be too similar in character — too easy-going to 'improve' each other); Mr and Mrs Gardiner (a good match, intelligent, cultured, supportive of each other, good companions and as a result good loving parents to their children); Mr Darcy and Elizabeth (they grow to become a good match, the novel shows how each makes the other moderate their pride and question their prejudices). Like the Gardiners, Darcy and Elizabeth are intelligent, cultured and good communicators both in

> **Key quotation**
>
> It is a truth universally acknowledged, that a single man in possession of a good fortune, must be in want of a wife.
>
> (Chapter 1, page 5)

spoken and written words. Theirs will be a marriage which offers love and companionship — and very good finances. A solid basis for a happy family life.

- The qualities we might look for in a happy marriage in the twenty-first century: love, companionship, sound finances, in that order, make the theme still relevant and interesting to readers today.
- Conclusion — what point is Austen making about marriage? No explicit message: she leaves the reader to work out the idea that, as well as money, mutual affection and mutual improvement make for happiness in marriage and in family life. This was not perhaps a typical view at that time in the social classes she writes about.

Interpreting the question

Sometimes the question is open to **interpretation**. In the example question discussed in the breakdown above, the main problem is the wide-ranging extent of the theme of marriage in the novel. A foundation-tier question could ask for a contrast of one good and one bad marriage, but here you are left to work out what to write for yourself.

In an interpretation question you need to plan your intended answer carefully to make sure you can write your answer in the time available (generally between 40 minutes and an hour.) In this case, for example, you might decide to focus on fewer marriages and go into more textual detail on each one.

The form of your plan

In an exam, the plan will have to be done quickly: no more than 5 minutes of jotting down ideas. You could use:

- a spider diagram or flow chart, allowing you to keep your mind open to new ideas: you can simply slot them in even as you are writing
- a list of ideas to include in each paragraph (like the notes above), but this may be more difficult to add to

For a controlled assessment, you will have more time to plan and prepare in class, possibly even working in groups and discussing your ideas. You will need to get the important points down on paper before you arrange them in the order you intend to write about them. On a spider diagram, arranging is a simple matter of numbering the ideas in the best order. When you sit down to write your assessment, you will not be able to use notes you have prepared earlier, so you will have to summarise your main ideas quickly from memory.

Answering a question using an extract

Some exam boards (WJEC, Edexcel and OCR) set exam questions based on an extract from the book. In this case, make good use of the material provided. Focus on the extract but not to the exclusion of all else — some of the questions may ask you to link ideas in the extract with material from other parts of the book.

Suppose you are answering the higher-tier question below, including an extract.

> Look closely at how Austen presents the character of Mr Darcy. How does it influence the reader's attitude towards him?

The extract is Chapter 3, pages 10–12, from 'Mr Bingley had soon made himself acquainted with all the principal people in the room...' to '... Elizabeth remained with no very cordial feelings towards him.'

Remember that you can **underline phrases** in the passage and **make notes in the margin** of the extract to follow up in your essay, as shown below.

> ### Grade *booster*
>
> Being able to suggest alternative interpretations of evidence is a feature of A-grade writing. Look beyond the obvious meaning of the words on the page and analyse the inferences.

Line from text	Comment
'What a contrast between him and his friend!' '...danced only once... declined being introduced to any other lady ...speaking occasionally to one of his own party.'	Darcy's behaviour is immediately contrasted with Bingley's: whereas Bingley is outgoing and friendly, Darcy is reserved and aloof.
'He was the proudest, most disagreeable man in the world,...'	The reader may interpret this as a sign that he is a snob, as the narrator explicitly implies, or could make the inference that he is shy amongst strangers.
'...I detest it [dancing], unless I am particularly acquainted with my partner...'	A clue for the attentive reader that Darcy is shy rather than proud.
'...there is not another woman in the room whom it would not be a punishment for me to stand up with.' 'She is tolerable, but not handsome enough to tempt *me*;'	Having just made eye-contact with Elizabeth, this is extremely impolite: Darcy must be aware that Elizabeth can hear him. These comments are not gentlemanly and prompt her negative feelings (prejudice) about him. The reader will agree with her judgement of Darcy at this point.
'Elizabeth had been obliged, by the scarcity of gentlemen, to sit down for two dances;' and '...young ladies who are slighted by other men.'	Further evidence of Darcy's poor manners: leaving a lady seated by choosing not to dance goes against the etiquette of the ballroom. Note irony: it is Darcy who is guilty of slighting Elizabeth, but too arrogant to understand that he is condemning his own rudeness. Elizabeth's response is to mock him; the reader will echo her ridicule of this pompous remark.

Structuring your essay

A well-planned essay has three sections:

1 beginning (introduction)
2 middle (development)
3 end (conclusion)

You need good ideas to write a good essay, which is why planning is so important, but you also need to demonstrate that you can put ideas together in a logical order, developing your argument to reach your conclusion. Here are some hints for each section of the essay.

Beginning (introduction)

Spending far too much time on an introduction is a common mistake. Instead, limit yourself to an opening paragraph of four or five sentences. This should:

- refer to the question and give an initial response to it
- show you have understood all aspects of the question
- show how you intend to answer it, hinting at the views you will put forward
- explain your interpretation, if there is more than one possible interpretation

You may need to give some contextual background. Do so by all means, but briefly.

Never begin 'In this essay I am going to...'. Your opening sentence should reflect the wording of the question in a punchy way. Do not write an introduction that is a list. It is much better to start as follows:

On his first appearance in the novel, Austen reveals the character of Mr Darcy to the reader in several ways, one of which is the inaccurate snap judgement of general opinion.

An opening sentence of this sort shows you have the question in focus and that you are aware that there are a variety of points to be made as you develop your answer.

Middle (development)

This part of the essay is easier than the other two. If you have a good plan, you know what you are doing by now. You can present your argument point by point with appropriate evidence to back it up. Your biggest challenge in this part of the essay is to make it flow smoothly from point to point, showing how the points connect.

Pause for thought

You only have 20 minutes to answer a WJEC extract question. If you are writing a short answer, how short do you think your introduction ought to be?

A good plan arranges your points in a logical way so that one leads on to the next. However, it is also important to use appropriate link words and connectives to signpost your ideas, giving the reader an idea of what is coming next and how it relates to the previous idea. The words and phrases in the table below will help, though it is important not to overuse connective words: try not to begin any two paragraphs in a row with the same one.

Word/phrase	Idea it contains
However/Yet	An exception is coming: '*However*, Mr Bennet hears a very different account of the ball from the one he had been hoping for.' *Yet* can also be used without the comma.
Despite this/ Nevertheless/ Nonetheless	Signals an apparent contradiction: '*Despite this*, Elizabeth reacts with good-humour, turning the insult into a source of ridicule.'
On the other hand	Signals a balanced alternative: '*On the other hand*, it could be argued that there is another explanation for Darcy's behaviour: he is shy rather than proud.' Useful for showing you realise that different interpretations of the text are valid.
By contrast	Compares two features. A paragraph about the 'amiable' qualities of Bingley could be followed with: '*By contrast*, Mr Darcy is aloof and cold.'
Similarly	Gives a similar example: '*Similarly*, the younger Bennet girls were delighted with their evening's entertainment.'
Another example	'*Another example* of Darcy's harsh judgement of his new neighbours is to be found in his reactions to the evening's entertainment at Lucas Lodge.'
In addition	'*In addition*, Darcy insults Elizabeth by describing her as 'tolerable, but not handsome…'
Above all	Introduces the most important of several points: '*Above all*, Darcy admires Elizabeth for her lively mind and her wit.'

End (conclusion)

The conclusion should draw your arguments to a logical close, not simply repeat them in a different form. If you have explored two or more sides of an argument, use the conclusion to state which side you take. For example, 'Having looked at both sides of this question, I feel that…'

Your conclusion must refer back to the question, showing you have not lost sight of it. Try to give an overview of your opinion: this will help the examiner to see your essay as a whole. You might include a quotation from the text in the last couple of lines, especially one that relates to the essay question. For example:

Having considered the evidence, I believe that the reader is likely to empathise with Elizabeth's reaction to Darcy's stand-offish behaviour and slighting words, having 'no very cordial feelings towards him'.

Using quotations and referring to the text

It is essential to use quotations and references to the text in your exam essay to provide evidence for your argument. You can express your personal views on the text — examiners will be delighted to read something original — but you must always back them up with detailed evidence.

Most exam boards allow books in the exam or controlled assessment (not annotated ones) so finding the quotations is a matter of knowing the text. Some exam boards, for example WJEC, do not allow texts, so for these exams you will have to learn a selection of key quotations.

Using quotations effectively comes down to five principles:

1 Inverted commas at the beginning and end of the quoted words.

2 Write the quotation exactly as it appears in the text (tricky if you are quoting from memory).

3 Do not repeat the exact words of the quotation as an explanation of it.

4 Use a quotation that fits into your sentence.

5 Keep quotations as short as possible (use ellipsis … to cut out unnecessary phrases).

> **Grade *booster*** !
>
> There is no need to tell the examiner that you are using a quotation (or, worse still, abbreviate the word to quote): there are quotation marks to make this clear. Instead, begin your explanation with a phrase such as 'This makes it sound as if/gives the impression/makes the reader think/conveys a sense of/creates a feeling of/reminds the reader of…'

Separate quotations

You may know these as PEE points, where you make your point, then give the evidence as a quotation on a separate line, followed by your comment explaining its significance:

When Wickham first appears he is planning to join the army:
'the young man wanted only regimentals to make him completely charming' which implies that he will be perfect once he is in army uniform.

Embedded quotations

An embedded quotation is one that runs on from your own words on the same line:

Jane's letters reinforce this point, at first judging Wickham as: 'thoughtless and indiscreet…nothing bad at heart', however, even Jane, who always thinks the best of everyone, agrees he is 'not a man to be trusted' when the whole story is told.

This kind of quotation works best if the sentence as a whole, with the quotation, is grammatically correct. Use brackets [...] to alter the verb tense or to replace a pronoun with a noun to make your quotation fit your sentence.

Referring to the text

It is not always necessary to use a quotation. If you cannot accurately recall or find the quotation you want, it is often just as good to refer to it:

In his letter Darcy reveals the truth: how Wickham rejected the offer of a career in the church and chose to study law instead, then wasted the £3,000 Darcy agreed to give him in place of the promised living.

If you are in an exam where you have no access to the text, this is better than misquoting your evidence. This technique is especially useful if you need to sum up a lengthy passage.

Referring to the author and title

Refer to Austen either by name or as 'the author'. You do not need to give her first name (Jane) — just Austen will do, but never refer to her as just 'Jane'.

You can save time by shortening the title. Give the title in full, plus the abbreviation, the first time you use it, for example '*Pride and Prejudice (P&P)*', then use the short version in the rest of your essay.

Writing in an appropriate style

Remember that you are expected to write in an appropriate style for a formal examination essay. Each year, examiners' reports list a range of inappropriate language used by candidates. These examples can make amusing reading, but they have lost the candidates marks. You must write in a suitable **register**. This means:

- not using colloquial language or slang (except when quoting dialogue): 'Mr Darcy is a right snob, so up himself he deserves for everyone to diss him'
- not becoming too personal or anecdotal: 'Charles reminds me of my Uncle Craig, life and soul of every party, like when my cousin Kelly got married he danced all night with everyone'
- using suitable phrases for an academic essay. For example, it is better to say 'It could be argued that...' rather than 'I reckon that...'. Much better to say: 'Bingley's words give the reader the impression that...' rather than 'This quote shows that...'

The first person ('I')

It used to be thought bad style to write essays in the first person (using 'I'). Now this is acceptable, although you should not do it all the way through the essay. You could use it to your advantage, especially in the opening and closing paragraphs, where you set out your argument and then give your considered opinion.

Review your learning

(Answers are given on page 93)

1. What is an essay?
2. What should you do to the question before attempting to answer it?
3. What are the three parts of an essay, and what should each part include?
4. What are the two ways to use quotations?
5. What other kind of textual evidence can you provide?
6. Explain three ways you can raise your grade towards an A. Which do you think you would be able to do in your essay?

More interactive questions and answers online.

Assessment Objectives and skills

- **What are Assessment Objectives?**
- **What are tiers?**
- **What will you get marks for?**
- **What will take up your time but gain you no marks?**

The examiner marking your exam essay, or the teacher who marks your controlled assessment, wants to give you marks, but can do so only if you succeed in fulfilling the key Assessment Objectives for English Literature. These are the same for all the English Literature specifications.
Candidates will be required to demonstrate their ability to:

- respond to texts critically and imaginatively; select and evaluate relevant textual detail to illustrate and support interpretations **(AO1)**
- explain how language, structure and form contribute to writers' presentation of ideas, themes and settings **(AO2)**
- make comparisons and explain links between texts, evaluating writers' different ways of expressing meaning and achieving effects **(AO3)**
- relate texts to their social, cultural and historical contexts; explain how texts have been influential and significant to self and other readers in different contexts and at different times **(AO4)**

Breaking down the Assessment Objectives

AO1

- **Candidates respond to texts critically:** means you must say what you think of the novel and why. Show you can analyse the text.
- **Imaginatively** means you are expected to show a creative, original response.
- You are asked to **select and evaluate relevant textual detail to illustrate and support interpretations**. This involves careful

choice of evidence from the text and giving your views on how effective the evidence is by analysis and evaluation.

AO2

- **Candidates explore how language, structure and form…:** the word 'language' refers to Austen's choice of words, or style. For example, when Elizabeth visits Pemberley, Austen emphasises the unspoilt beauty of the grounds by use of phrases like: '…a stream of some natural importance… without any artificial appearance. … neither formal nor falsely adorned' (page 187). These details do more than just describe, they make a judgement about Darcy's character and taste; the choice of language communicates an abstract idea. The word 'structure' refers to the overall shape of the novel, as discussed in the *Plot and structure* section (pages 26–27): the plot unfolds over a year with a link between the events and the seasons. The word 'form' is concerned with the genre of the text: Austen chooses to write in the form of a novel, rather than, say, a play script, but she is influenced by the form of the epistolary novel (see page 61) and she is contributing to the form of the modern romantic novel.

Grade *booster*

Knowing what the Assessment Objectives are, and which ones are tested in your exam, will help you to get the best possible marks for your essay.

- **…contribute to writers' presentation of ideas, themes and settings:** means you to have to show how language, structure and form shape the meaning of the text. Ideas and themes are the big messages of the novel explored in the *Themes* section, for example what information Austen includes to make the reader think about marriage and family life. How she writes about settings is indicated above and explored further in the *Style* section, page 64.

AO3

- **Make comparisons and explain links between texts** means that you are expected to be able to show what differences there are between two texts, or what they have in common. This is not expected in exam questions. Some controlled assessment tasks, for example those set by AQA and CCEA, do require comparison of two literary heritage texts, the second of which is a play by Shakespeare.

Here is an example question:

> Compare how *Romeo and Juliet* and *Pride and Prejudice* reveal the relationship between Juliet and her parents, and between Elizabeth Bennet and her parents.

You would need to investigate and evaluate evidence from both these texts.

- **Evaluating writers' different ways of expressing meaning** links with AO2: you have to make comparisons between aspects of each author's writing, such as style, form and structure.
- The words **achieving effects** focus your attention on the impact of the text on the reader. You will be comparing the judgements you make: how the plot, or the style, engages you by use of humour, excitement or shock; the extent to which the writer makes you feel dislike of or sympathy with characters.

AO4

- **Candidates relate texts to their social, cultural and historical contexts:** this is important when you are studying a literary heritage text such as *Pride and Prejudice* for two reasons: first because it was written nearly two centuries ago, second because it is a significant influence on later authors. Understanding of the context in which Austen wrote the novel includes:
  - **the social and historical context**, the world of Regency England and the particular restrictions on Austen's writing that arise from her social class and her gender
  - **the cultural context**, the influence of previous writers on Austen's work, (for example those who pioneered the novel genre) and the Romantic movement (with its revolutionary ideas of social and gender equality). You will not be expected to compare *Pride and Prejudice* with specific novels from Austen's time. However, knowing that she was a keen reader and what an epistolary novel is could be relevant.
- **Explain how texts have been influential and significant to self and other readers in different contexts and at different times** means that you are able to comment on how nineteenth century readers may have responded to the text. These readers would have understood the manners and social requirements of the novel's world, which may seem strange to readers today. You should be able to comment on the relevance of the novel to your world and understand that the gender, class or ethnic background of modern readers may lead to some seeing more relevance in Austen's concerns than others. For example women generally read more romances than men; a reader who has a strong Christian or Islamic faith may find particular relevance in the emphasis on the importance of marriage and family to the status of a woman.

> **Pause for thought**
>
> Do you know which exam board will be assessing your work? Do you know which AOs get you marks? Read this section carefully so that your writing covers the appropriate content.

How AOs apply to different exam boards

There is quite a difference between the proportion of marks given to each AO by the different exam boards, and this will be reflected in the questions they set.

- AO1 is important for all exam boards. AQA, Edexcel and OCR award half the marks in this exam question for showing detailed knowledge and understanding of the novel whereas WJEC only gives one third of the marks to this AO.
- AO2 is important for AQA, OCR and, with fewer marks allocated, for Edexcel, but response to language is not tested on this question by WJEC.
- AO3 gains marks where *Pride and Prejudice* is tested linked to another text by controlled assessment. For AQA it is possible to do *Pride and Prejudice* as part of a Linked Text controlled assignment where marks are given for comparison; in this case fewer marks are given for AO1 (detailed knowledge and understanding) than in an answer on *Pride and Prejudice* in the AQA exam. For CCEA, linked controlled assessment is the only test of Literary Heritage prose.
- AO4 contributes a small proportion of marks to AQA and Edexcel exams but is central to WJEC English literature where understanding of context accounts for two-thirds of the marks. It is also worth more than one third of the marks on the CCEA controlled assessment.

What you will not get marks for

The Assessment Objectives tell you what you *will* get marks for. It is also important to know what you *will not* get marks for:

- **Retelling the story**. You can be certain that the examiner marking your essay already knows the plot of *Pride and Prejudice*. The examiner follows a mark scheme and will probably be referring to 'grade descriptors' — these outline the features to be expected from essays at each of the grades. A key feature of the lowest grades, as identified by the grade descriptors, is 'retelling the story'.
- **Quoting long passages**. You will waste time and gain no marks by quoting long passages from the novel. Where books are available in the exam, it is a temptation for those who have not prepared thoroughly to make answers longer by copying out chunks of the text — or the extract given for extract-based questions. It wastes time and doesn't get marks. Use your judgement: it is rarely necessary to quote more than two sentences at a time.

- **Identifying figures of speech or other features.** You will never gain marks simply for identifying images such as similes or metaphors. Similarly, you will gain no marks for pointing out that 'Austen uses a lot of adjectives in this passage'.
- **Giving unsubstantiated opinions.** The examiner will be keen to give you marks for your opinions but only if they are supported by reasoned argument and references to the text (see AO1 above.) Therefore, you will get no marks for writing 'Everyone thinks that Lydia is completely stupid but I don't.' You will get marks for 'It is easy to dismiss Lydia as having a complete lack of sense and judgement, however, she does show a capacity for fun and enjoyment of life which reflects that of her older sister Elizabeth. Unfortunately she does not have Elizabeth's intellect, neither does she have the guidance from her parents that her immaturity calls for.'

Grade **booster**

You will gain marks by *identifying language features* and then going on to say:
- *why* the author has used them
- *how effective* you think they are

Foundation and higher tiers

You will be entered for the examination at either the foundation or the higher tier.

Foundation tier

Foundation tier can get you a grade between C and G. The questions are easier than those for the higher tier, usually based on plot and character rather than themes or style and asking for less in the way of content. For example, higher-tier questions might ask for two characters to be compared where the foundation paper will just ask for your opinion of one. Most exam boards provide bullet points to guide your answer: make sure you think about these hints and make use of them. They are helpful as the basis of your essay plan (see page 68).

The skills you need for either tier are the same, but if you know you are being entered for the foundation tier, be especially careful not to do any of the things listed above under the heading *What you will not get marks for*. Remember the highest grade you can get is a C.

Sample foundation-tier type questions

OCR, Edexcel and WJEC set extract-based questions. For WJEC you have to complete this as well as a longer answer for an essay question. For OCR and Edexcel you can choose it instead of the essay.

Grade **booster**

Beware! Where there is a choice, some candidates will choose the extract question because it looks easier. If it is the only question you do, it will require you to show knowledge of other parts of the novel as well as the extract printed on the exam paper.

OCR-type extract question

Read from 'This is not to be borne! Miss Bennet...' to '...you would not wish to quit the sphere in which you have been brought up' (pages 273–74).

What makes Lady Catherine such an unpleasant character in this extract?

You should consider:
- her attitude to Elizabeth
- her opinion of herself and her importance
- the words and phrases she and Elizabeth use. *(15 marks)*

Edexcel-type extract question

Read from 'Elizabeth's impatience to acquaint Jane with what had happened could no longer be overcome...' to '"And poor Mr Darcy! Dear Lizzy, only consider what he must have suffered"' (pages 173–74).

Answer all parts of the question that follows as fully as possible.

(a) Outline the key events from this extract up to when Lydia and Wickham are found living in London. *(10 marks)*

(b) From this extract, what do you learn about Elizabeth's character? Use examples from the extract to support your answer. *(10 marks)*

(c) Comment on Elizabeth and Jane's attitudes to men in the extract. *(10 marks)*

(d) Explain Elizabeth's attitudes to men in one other part of the novel. Use examples to support your answer. *(10 marks)*

(Total: 40 marks)

WJEC-type extract question

What do you think of the way Mr Darcy speaks and behaves here?
Give reasons for what you say, and remember to support your answer with words and phrases from the extract. *(10 marks)*

(The extract is Chapter 3, pages 10–12, from 'Mr Bingley had soon made himself acquainted...' to '...Elizabeth remained with no very cordial feelings towards him.')

Notice that the wording of the question above is slightly different from that of the higher-tier question on p. 82, though the extract is the same.

AQA-style character question

Answer **both** parts (a) and (b).

(a) What different impressions do you have of Mr Wickham in different parts of the novel? Remember to write about the society he lives in. *(12 marks)*

(b) How does Austen's way of writing create this impression of Mr Wickham? *(12 marks)*

WJEC-style theme question

There are successful and some unsuccessful marriages in *Pride and Prejudice*.

Choose **either** a successful **or** an unsuccessful marriage.

Write about the marriage you have chosen, explaining why you find it interesting. *(20 marks)*

Higher tier

Higher-tier questions may not give bullet-point hints to help you. If they do, think about the points and use them as a beginning for your essay plan but make sure you add your own ideas. Simply writing a paragraph on each bullet point will not produce a well-structured essay. Otherwise, you need to think carefully about what the question is really asking you to do.

You may also find, especially for AQA, that your question is more sophisticated than those on the foundation-tier paper. In particular, you may be asked to write about themes or style, not just about character. However, a more demanding question is more likely to offer bullet-point hints. Below are some examples of higher-tier type questions. Compare them with the foundation-tier questions above to see how they demand more of the exam candidate.

Remember the grades you can get on a higher-tier paper go from D to A*. If you don't get enough marks for a D grade, you will be unclassified.

Sample higher-tier type questions

OCR-type extract question

(Extract pages 273–74 as on p. 80).

How does Austen make you respect Elizabeth and dislike Lady Catherine as you read this extract? *(24 marks)*

Edexcel-type extract question

(Extract pages 173–74 as on p. 80).

Answer all parts of the question that follows as fully as possible.
(a) From this extract, what do you learn about Jane's character?
   Use examples from the extract to support your answer. *(10 marks)*
(b) Comment in detail on the attitudes of Elizabeth and Jane to men in the extract. *(10 marks)*
(c) Explain Elizabeth's attitudes to men as shown in **one other** part of the novel.
   Use examples to support your answer. *(10 marks)*
(d) How is Elizabeth's relationship with Darcy presented in **one other** part of the novel?
   Use examples to support your answer. *(10 marks)*
   (Total: 40 marks)

WJEC-style extract question
Look closely at how Austen presents the character of Mr Darcy. How does it influence the reader's attitude towards him?

(The extract is the same as for the foundation-tier question on page 80.)

OCR-style character question
How does Austen make Mr Collins a humorous character in *Pride and Prejudice*?

WJEC-style theme question
How does Austen present the theme of marriage in *Pride and Prejudice*?

AQA-style theme question
Referring to the relationship between Mr Bingley and Jane and between Mr Collins and Charlotte Lucas, what positive and negative aspects of marriage does Austen present in *Pride and Prejudice*?
Remember to write about the society they live in.

AQA-style character/theme question
Explore the growth of the relationship between Elizabeth and Darcy.
In your answer, remember to write about the society they live in.

You may include other ideas of your own.   *(Total: 40 marks)*

Review your learning

(Answers are given on page 94)

1. How many Assessment Objectives are there and what is each one about?

2. What are tiers? What grade can you get from each tier?

3. What gets marks in an exam?

4. What wastes time and gets you few marks?

More interactive questions and answers online.

Sample essays

- **What features does a C-grade essay have?**
- **How does an A-grade essay improve on that?**
- **What should you include in a good introduction and conclusion?**
- **What is an 'appropriate' essay style?**

Two sample essays are provided below: grade C and grade A* answers to a character-based question. Read the grade C essay first and think how you could improve it. Then read the A* essay. Remember that there could be many different good approaches to the same essay. These sample essays are not meant to be learnt by heart and reproduced in the exam.

Foundation tier

> **(a)** What different impressions do you have of Mr Wickham in different parts of the novel?
> Remember to write about the society he lives in. *(12 marks)*
>
> **(b)** How does Austen's way of writing create this impression of Mr Wickham? *(12 marks)*

Grade C answer

(a) George Wickham is a character introduced early on in the novel as a rival to Darcy, but as the story goes on we learn that he is not what he first seems to be. To begin with Elizabeth is taken in by his good looks and chat, until she finds out more. There is no clue at all**1** to what he is really like.

When he first appears he is planning to join the army:

'...the young man wanted only regimentals to make him completely charming.'**2**

This shows he will be completely perfect once he is in an army uniform.

There is one weird moment when Darcy appears and he goes white**3** but you can't work out why.

He talks to Elizabeth a lot after this and Elizabeth trusts him. It says he talks with 'gallantry'**4** which implies he is a very pleasant man and the very opposite of Darcy. This makes the story he tells of Darcy's selfishness and greed more significant.

1 Not necessarily true — C grade because it fails to read between the lines

2 Good quoted evidence, contextual relevance could be mentioned

3 Poorly worded — ambiguous as to which of the two goes white

4 Incomplete understanding — in 1800, gallantry implied an eye for the ladies and the 'warm temper' alludes to his being quick to anger

'...a dislike which I cannot but attribute in some measure to jealousy.'

He says that the late Mr Darcy intended to 'provide amply' for him but that Darcy got all the money by fault**5**. This makes Darcy out to be the bad guy to the reader and makes Wickham sound like the victim. Wickham says he has a 'warm unguarded temper'**4** which also make him sound favourable and a contrast to Darcy.

5 Wrong word — and the sentence that follows is inappropriate in style

The first clue we get that he is not what Elizabeth hoped is when he gets engaged to Miss King, who has inherited some money. That seems fair enough as he doesn't have any of his own and in those days, in that class, people had to have money to get married.**6** However, when Darcy writes what Wickham really did and how he chose to go into the law instead of the church, then wasted the £1,000 Mr Darcy had left to him by:

6 Some indication of understanding of social context but undeveloped

'a life of idleness and dissipation'

from this it is obvious why Darcy did not let him have the position his father promised.**7**

7 A good point made here, but the sum of money is inaccurate, expression is clumsy and the paragraph doesn't have the impact it could have

Worse than that, he tried to run off with Darcy's sister and she was only fifteen. He was obviously after her money, just as he was with Miss King, who is soon whisked away from him by her relatives to go a long way away to Liverpool, where it would take days to get to.**8**

8 Slipping into story telling and irrelevance

Elizabeth's big mistake is that she doesn't let anyone except Jane know any of this, so no one thinks twice when Lydia keeps talking about him, and then she is allowed to go to Brighton when his regiment goes there.**9**

9 Story telling — losing focus of the title — Wickham

Next thing we know, Elizabeth gets a letter from Jane saying that Wickham and Lydia have eloped to Gretna Green to get married, but he is even worse than that, he just goes to live with Lydia in London, which would have been extremely shocking in those days, as respectable unmarried couples did not live together.**10**

10 Again, social context hinted at but undeveloped

Fortunately, Darcy finds them and gives Wickham shedloads of money**11** to pay off all his gambling debts and persuade him to marry Lydia. He has no shame at all and acts as if he never did anything wrong:

11 Poor expression: 'shedloads'. Could do with evidence.

'We were always good friends and now are better'**12**

12 A good piece of evidence, but the analysis needs development

This is what he says to Elizabeth, who he really flirted with at the start and he must know it is not right to marry her sister without even apologising. They talk about her visit to Pemberley and if she met Darcy's sister. She asks him if he would have liked giving sermons.

'Exceedingly well. I should have considered it as part of my duty and the exertion would soon have been nothing. One ought not to repine; but to be sure, it would have been such a thing for me!'**13**

13 Interesting quotation but overlong — needs cutting

He must know that she has heard the truth about him, but still doesn't say anything to excuse himself.**14**

The last time he is mentioned is at the very end when it says he is always in debt so he and Lydia depend on Elizabeth and Darcy for money and Bingley and Jane for somewhere to live. My impression of him is really bad and completely different from the 'gentleman' I thought he was to start with.**15**

(b) The way Austen writes about Wickham is quite clever as she keeps you guessing by fooling you into thinking he is just the man for Elizabeth, then gradually showing the truth.

She uses dialogue to show what a good persuasive talker he is and how he shows himself in a good light by using positive emotive words:

'He was my godfather and excessively attached to me. I cannot do justice to his kindness. He meant to provide for me amply, and thought he had done it…'

Words like this make you believe that Darcy was jealous of how his father favoured Wickham.

He is shown as a big contrast to Darcy, very friendly and trusting to tell so much about himself. It also says how attractive Elizabeth found him: '…whose very countenance may vouch for your being amiable'. The fact that he is saying negative things about Darcy that Elizabeth wants to hear to match her prejudice makes him even more attractive to her.

The bad things about Wickham are all told by other people and a lot of it is in letters. Elizabeth's aunt warns her that getting too attached to him is a waste of time because they could not afford to marry, so when they discuss Miss King, you just go along and agree with Elizabeth that he did what he had to do. Only when Darcy tells her in the letter he writes about how he wasted his inheritance and what happened with Georgiana, you begin to realise he is a real villain and not to be trusted at all.

Jane's letters all about Lydia make this point too. At first she just says he is:

'thoughtless and indiscreet…nothing bad at heart'

But when the whole truth comes out, even Jane, who always thinks the best of everyone, says he is 'not a man to be trusted'.

When Mrs Gardiner's letter tells the whole truth about how much it cost Darcy to persuade Wickham to marry Lydia, then it is clear he is a real villain with no morals and no feelings.

Debts paid '…amounting…to considerably more than a thousand pounds, another thousand…settled on her and his commission purchased.'

14 More analysis required. For example, his comments about Georgiana seem inappropriate given that she is the girl he persuaded to love him and with whom he attempted to elope.

15 Attempt at conclusion — sums up that there is a change in impression but no detail about what it is. Needs to refer back to the question more explicitly

This list shows just how much of a fortune hunter Wickham is.

The way he talks to Elizabeth at the end, as if nothing has happened, just shows what a hypocrite he is.

Austen's method of fooling us into thinking he is really good, then gradually showing all the other evidence to shock us made him an interesting character.

Like the answer to part (a), this is also clearly a C-grade answer. It does focus on the task set — here a more complex one that involves looking at the writer's style. Each section generally manages to avoid storytelling and selects evidence from the text to support the points made. Both parts are sustained at some length. In part (b) there is an attempt to get to grips with language (emotive words, use of lists) as well as different narrative methods such as dialogue and letters.

The two main reasons that this answer is a C-grade one are:

- the simple level of analysis
- the inappropriate style

To get to the higher grades, more than accuracy is required. You need to demonstrate the sophistication of your understanding.

Higher tier

What different impressions do you have of Mr Wickham in different parts of the novel, and how does Austen create this impression? Remember to write about the society he lives in. *(24 marks)*

Grade A* answer

1 Strong introduction — refers to both parts of the question, making an important observation relating to the novel's original title and hinting at understanding of a central theme. This initial opinion is developed in the essay.

2 Awareness of authorial methods

3 Selects good evidence and makes a sophisticated critical judgement

George Wickham is introduced early on in the novel as a rival for Elizabeth's affection, though right from the outset it is hinted that he is not what he seems to be. Austen's narrative method is engaging for the reader as she keeps us guessing whether to agree with Elizabeth that he is just the man for her, or whether her 'first impression' of him is as misguided as that of Darcy.**1**

The description which introduces Wickham has elements of irony:**2** he is described as having a 'most gentlemanlike appearance' and ... [wanting] only regimentals to make him completely charming' which alerts the reader into questioning whether his appearance may be deceptive. A soldier's uniform might well make him look very handsome to a certain shallow type of girl, but the man beneath matters more than his 'charming' appearance.**3**

Authorial comment proclaims him to have ' a happy readiness of conversation... perfectly correct and unassuming' in direct contrast to the taciturn Mr Darcy, though he goes oddly silent when Darcy appears and 'Both changed colour, one looked white, the other red,' which arouses curiosity as to what has happened between the two.

When he next meets Elizabeth at her aunt's gathering, Austen makes extensive use of dialogue**4** to show how articulate and persuasive he can be, and how he shows himself in a good light by gaining sympathy both from the reader and Elizabeth. He begins by fuelling her prejudice against Darcy claiming that 'The world is blinded by his fortune and consequence, or frightened by his high and imposing manners…'**5** Encouraged by Elizabeth's response, he continues in this negative vein to imply that he has been hard done by, a 'disappointed man' as the church 'ought' to have been his profession.

4 Another technique mentioned: focuses on the question

5 Good use of short quotations with an explanation of their significance

He relates how the late Mr Darcy intended to 'provide amply' for him with a 'valuable living'.**6** This is very significant, because it was normally the second son of a wealthy family who was given the opportunity to enter the church, however Wickham was merely the son of one of the employees on the estate, so this was a real act of generosity.**7** When he claims that Darcy denied him this promise because of 'a dislike which I cannot but attribute in some measure to jealousy', the reader may well surmise that this could be the truth. However there are plenty of clues here that Wickham caused his own problems: he says Darcy accused him of 'extravagance, imprudence – in short anything or nothing' and confesses to a 'warm unguarded temper' and, though these are fairly abstract as descriptions of any faults, they do turn out to be at the root of the actions which led to Darcy's decision not to honour his father's promise.**8** One reason Elizabeth believes him is how attractive she finds him: his '…very countenance may vouch for [his] being amiable'. She is also blind to how inappropriate such intimate revelations are to a person he hardly knows, largely because of her prejudice against Darcy.

6 Shows clear understanding of complex content

7 Linked with sophisticated knowledge about historical context

8 Perceptive inference and interpretation with good use of apt short quotations

Elizabeth continues to enjoy his company for a couple of months, until her aunt Gardiner warns her not to become too attached to him since they could never afford to marry, so when they hear of his engagement to a Miss King, who has inherited a fortune of £10,000, with thoughts of Charlotte Lucas's 'sensible' choice, the reader sides with Elizabeth that Wickham achieved what he needed. In Regency England, the upper classes sometimes married just for money and certainly rarely married without considering the financial side of things.**9** However damning information, often from this point on communicated in letters, (a technique Austen uses to propel her narrative)**10** indicates that Wickham has very few scruples when it comes to money. After Elizabeth has rejected Darcy's proposal of marriage, partly on the grounds of his mistreatment of Wickham, he reveals the truth: how Wickham rejected the offer of a career in the church and chose to study law instead, then wasted the £3,000 Darcy agreed to give him in place of the promised living on 'a

9 Understanding of context integrated with detailed knowledge of the text

10 Reference to authorial methods

life of idleness and dissipation', instead of spending it on his studies as he claimed he would.

The same letter also reveals that Miss King is not the first heiress to tempt him, for he planned an elopement with Georgiana Darcy when she was only fifteen years old. Fortunately, like Miss King, Georgiana was rescued before any harm was done.**10** Elizabeth tells no one except Jane about any of this, so warning signs are missed when Lydia, with a crush on Wickham, is allowed to follow his regiment on its new posting to Brighton. Not much more than a month later, Elizabeth is shocked to be informed in two letters from Jane that Wickham and Lydia have eloped to Scotland, then, even worse, that they are unmarried and living together in London. Add this to the tale of Miss King and Georgiana and it is evident that Wickham is an unscrupulous villain.

11 Refers to the question and gives a personal opinion supported by good textual knowledge and well-chosen brief quotation

Jane's letters reinforce this point too, at first judging him as: 'thoughtless and indiscreet … nothing bad at heart', however, even Jane, who always thinks the best of everyone, agrees he is 'not a man to be trusted' when the whole story is told.**11**

12 Sophisticated grasp of social and historical context

Fortunately, Darcy finds them and the couple are married. This is a huge relief to Elizabeth as the scandal would have made the whole family social outcasts at that time, not to speak of the consequences for Lydia, who may well have slipped into a life of prostitution, as there would have been little hope of any other future for her once Wickham lost interest.**12**

13 Good textual detail to make a clear point

The complete tale of Wickham's moral evil is not revealed until Mrs Gardiner's letter communicates what Darcy paid Wickham to marry Lydia: his debts paid 'amounting…to considerably more than a thousand pounds, another thousand… settled on her and his commission purchased.'**13** Darcy even has the forethought to buy him a position in a regiment stationed hundreds of miles north in Newcastle, well away from gossip about the seedy start to their marriage.

14 Reaching judgements about the character — focus on task

15 Good use of short quotations to illustrate elements of irony

When the newly-weds visit her family before leaving for their new life, Wickham shows himself to be shameless, saying to Elizabeth, 'We were always good friends and now are better.' The hypocrisy of the man who, less than a year before, offered himself as far more than a 'friend' and who has now married her sister in such disgraceful circumstances is breath-taking!**14** They talk about Pemberley and there is veiled mention of Darcy's sister ('When I last saw her she was not very promising.') and of Wickham's thwarted ambitions in the Church, ('I should have considered [giving sermons] part of my duty and the exertion would soon have been nothing.')**15**

He must know that she has heard the truth about him, but makes no attempt to defend himself.

Austen concludes by summing up the life he goes on to lead. He soon loses interest in Lydia, but retains the hope, despite all the evil he has done, and all he already owes to Darcy, that 'Darcy might yet be prevailed upon to make his fortune.' Their 'extravagant' and 'heedless' lifestyle leads them to depend on Elizabeth and Darcy for money and Bingley and Jane for somewhere to live.**16**

16 Sums up neatly

Wickham is a perfect illustration of the theme which shows how deceptive appearances can be. Austen's method of allowing the reader to uncover the depths of his villainy alongside Elizabeth and to share her condemnation of the man who initially struck her as 'completely charming' is an interesting aspect of the novel.**17** He ends, as he began, a total contrast to Darcy, whose good qualities are emphasised by the comparison.

17 Conclusion illustrates clear focus on requirement of task

This is clearly a good A-grade answer. The task set is complex, combining a discussion of Wickham's character with investigation of the writer's style. The answer is focused, logical and very fluently expressed. Textual evidence supports all the points made and the quality of analysis and evaluation is high. There is detailed and relevant comment on social and historical context. It also shows a sophisticated grasp of authorial methods, such as use of dialogue and letters as well as choice of language.

In addition, it alludes to several of the themes in the novel, though this is not specifically required by the question. This essay demonstrates an overview of the whole text.

Review your learning

(Answers are given on page 94)

1. What main differences can you see between a C-grade and an A-grade essay?
2. What should your introduction and conclusion mention?
3. What does 'writing in an appropriate style' mean?

More interactive questions and answers online.

Answers

Answers to 'Review your learning' questions.

Context (p. 12)

1 The context of a novel includes the social, historical, cultural and literary factors which influenced the author, and the ways different readers respond to the novel.

2 Austen lived for only 41 years (1775–1817.) This is surprising, because, although life expectancy was lower, it was usually the lower classes who died so young. Despite her short life, she wrote six major novels which assured her reputation as the first great English woman novelist.

3 The Regency period was named for the Prince Regent, who ruled England from 1811, when his father George III was declared insane, until his death in 1820. The term is used for the time between the Georgian and the Victorian age: mid 1790s to 1830s.

4 Historical events during Austen's life included the French Revolution, and the Battle of Waterloo. The USA also gained independence from England. Look again at the list on page 8. Little reflection of any of these events is found in *Pride and Prejudice*, because women were not expected to concern themselves with such matters. However, the regiment is in Meryton because of the Napoleonic wars, and some relationships in the novel show that class distinctions are blurring.

5 A marriage based on romantic love is Austen's contribution to the genre of romantic fiction. For that reason, the novel has a timeless appeal. The issue of the importance of marriage for a girl and of parents wishing to find suitable husbands for their daughters still has relevance to some British communities: British Asians, for example, may find much that still feels familiar today in the attitudes expressed in *Pride and Prejudice*.

Plot and structure (p. 28)

1 The novel begins in September, possibly in 1799, and ends in October the following year.

2 You could have several different items in this list, but you may well have included: Elizabeth's initial dislike of Darcy, the social distance between his and her families, rivals for her affection, Wickham's lies about Darcy, Darcy's decision to separate Bingley from Jane, Lydia's elopement, Lady Catherine's disapproval, to name but a few.

3 Rivals for the heroine's affections are a typical feature of a romantic novel. Mr Collins shows that Elizabeth is not so desperate that she would

accept anyone's proposal; Wickham shows that she is able to attract a charmer, but turns out to be a villain; Darcy's own cousin, Colonel Fitzwilliam, is a genuine rival whose attentions to Elizabeth make Darcy jealous, though his circumstances mean the relationship has no future.

4 The Gardiners are important as the means of getting Elizabeth to Darcy's estate at Pemberley, where Elizabeth falls in love with him. They also show that high social class is not the only source of culture and good breeding. They represent the breaking down of social barriers when they become valued friends of the Darcys at the end. They serve as a contrast to Elizabeth's ineffective parents, at several times in the novel taking on a parental role for Elizabeth, Jane and Lydia, which is important to the plot as well as to the novel's themes.

5 Both Lydia and Georgiana are victims of Wickham. His plans to elope with Georgiana are discovered and prevented, however he succeeds in his plan with Lydia.

6 The seasons over the year of the novel act as a symbol for characters' emotions: after an exciting autumn, the winter months are quiet and slow, reflecting the unfulfilled hopes of Jane (with Bingley) and Elizabeth (with Wickham); Easter brings new life and hope as Darcy proposes to Elizabeth and her feelings towards him begin to grow; in the heat of the summer, love blooms at Pemberley; as the year of the novel comes to an end, the double marriage of Jane and Elizabeth in the autumn completes the cycle of the seasons.

7 Certain months see a great deal of action and activity: November is a time of excitement and anticipation in Longbourn, April, around Easter sees the renewal of Darcy's courtship, and in August, the events at Pemberley draw the reader in.

Characterisation (p. 45)

1 Characters can be revealed by any of the following: **conversation** — what a character says (or thinks) and what others say about them; **actions** — what a character does; **behaviour** in a social setting — words and actions relating to others; **authorial comment** —how the author explains or judges the character.

2 Mary, Kitty and Lydia Bennet are included as comparisons with Elizabeth. Lydia contributes to the plot by eloping with Wickham. All show stereotypical aspects of female behaviour, which adds humour to the novel.

3 Mr Collins and Lady Catherine de Bourgh are exaggerated caricatures. They add humour to the novel, but they also contribute to various themes (for instance by their pride) so they help the reader think about more than just the story.

4 **a** Jane Bennet   **d** Lydia Bennet
   b Mr Darcy   **e** Anne de Bourgh
   c Elizabeth Bennet

5 **a** Caroline Bingley to Darcy; shows her jealousy of his attention to Elizabeth and her snobbishness about Elizabeth's family — which she assumes he shares.
   b Mr Bennet to Mary; shows his witty cynicism as he draws attention to Mary's piano playing as being anything other than a 'delight' .
   c Lady Catherine to Elizabeth and other guests at Rosings; shows her self-centred boastful vanity as she claims excellence — for self and daughter — at something she has not even attempted.
   d Mrs Bennet to Elizabeth. Shows how materialistic she is: she is not concerned about whether her daughter actually likes the man she has agreed to marry, simply that she will gain money and possessions from the match.
   e Darcy to Elizabeth. Shows how deeply she has changed him by her comments that implied he had not behaved like a gentleman — how his reflections have led him to question his behaviour and to lose his earlier arrogance.

Themes (p. 56)

1 The themes identified are money and marriage, parenthood and family life, love and friendship, pride and prejudice, appearance and reality, social and moral codes.
2 The Bennets, the Lucases and the Gardiners are the main marriages used to illustrate the theme of family life.
3 Both Darcy and Wickham demonstrate that appearance may be deceptive.
4 The theme associated with context is social and moral codes.
5 The theme of marriage is closely connected with money because that was the reality of the time Austen was writing. The novel shows that the ideal includes love too, but sound finances are non-negotiable as a basis for upper class marriage.
6 You could make a case for most of the themes in this guide. If, for example, you chose marriage and money, you could argue:
   ● the first sentence of the book shows it is central
   ● the plot revolves around the four marriages in the novel
   ● there is a great deal of discussion of the need to marry with money in mind, for instance Elizabeth and Mrs Gardiner, Colonel Fitzwilliam and Elizabeth
   ● Lydia's marriage is only secured by outlay of money

Style (p. 65)

1 An epistolary novel is one made up entirely of letters between characters. *First Impressions*, an early draft of *Pride and Prejudice*, may have been written in this form. Around 30 letters are either mentioned, or included, in this novel.

2 Dialogue reveals characters through the subject matter and the style of speech. Mr Bennet's witty cynicism is unmistakable. Collins' strange mixture of vanity and humility is also characteristic.

3 Techniques used to incorporate humour include **exaggeration/ caricature** of characters, **satire** and **irony**.

4 The novel is written in the third person, though Austen, as **omniscient narrator**, sometimes chooses to interpret events through perceptions of different characters. When she writes ironically, there are elements of being an **unreliable narrator**. Letters also give the opportunity of including a variety of **first person viewpoints** of writers such as Darcy or Mrs Gardiner.

5 Symbolism is to be found in the way the seasons reflect the development of the plot. The description of Pemberley symbolises aspects of Darcy's character.

6 Instead of imagery, Austen chooses vocabulary with great care and describes characters' actions, thoughts and reactions with well-constructed phrases, sometimes using contrasts, or specifying what is *not* the case about a character. Caricature and satire play a part in this.

Tackling the assessments (p. 74)

1 The word 'essay' means 'an attempt' and puts a person's thoughts on a particular topic into writing.

2 Before starting to write, break down the title and plan your answer.

3 A good essay follows a predictable structure:
- an **introduction**, which shows you have understood what the task is about and suggests what you might have to say about it
- the **main body** of the essay, where your ideas are presented in a logical sequence of paragraphs
- a **conclusion**, where you sum up your final thoughts and the major reasons for them

4 Quotations can be separate or embedded (run on from your own words).

5 References to events or passages that you do not quote directly.

6 A-grade marks can be gained from:
- including alternative interpretations
- using the full range of ways of referring to evidence from the text

- analysing ideas and features of style in real detail — the word used in the assessment objectives is 'evaluating'
- including relevant information about context if your exam board gives marks for that
- planning carefully so that your answer in both full and logically structured
- writing in an appropriate, formal style

Read the section again if you were struggling with an answer to these questions.

Assessment Objectives and skills (p. 82)

1 There are four objectives:
  - AO1 Showing understanding of the text
  - AO2 About language
  - AO3 About comparisons
  - AO4 About context
2 Two tiers — Foundation grades G–C, Higher grades D–A*
3 You will be awarded marks for showing your ability to reach the grade descriptions for each of the Assessment Objectives your exam board sets out to test. Bear in mind that the examiner will have a mark scheme using 'grade descriptors' (a summary of the skills expected) and a list of possible content that candidates are likely to include at different grades. You can look at examples online at your exam board's website.
4 Do not:
  - retell the story
  - quote long passages
  - identify figures of speech without discussing their effectiveness
  - give unsubstantiated opinions

Sample essays (p. 89)

1 An A-grade essay has a clear focus on the task and provides a logically constructed, detailed answer selecting evidence from the whole novel.
  - Quotations are short and analysis is thoughtful.
  - Context is commented upon rather than just mentioned.
  - Writer's style and themes are commented on.
  - The written style of A-grade answer is fluent throughout.
  - An A-grade answer shows overview of text.
2 The introduction and conclusion should mention the task and show understanding of it.
3 Writing in a fairly formal way, without using colloquial language or slang.